A Practical Parrot (

Parrot Toys
& Play Areas

How to Put Some Fun into Your Parrot's Life

Carol S. D'Arezzo
Lauren Shannon-Nunn

CrowFire Publishing
Springfield, Virginia

This book contains the opinions and ideas of its authors. It is intended to provide helpful and informative material on the subject matter covered. It is sold with the understanding that the authors and publisher are not engaged in rendering professional services in the book. If the reader requires personal assistance or advice, a competent professional should be consulted.

The authors and publisher specifically disclaim any responsibility for any liability, loss, or risk, personal or otherwise, which is incurred as a consequence, directly or indirectly, of the use and application of any of the contents of this book. We assume no responsibility for errors, inaccuracies, omissions, or any other inconsistencies herein.

Published by CrowFire Publishing, PO Box 2456, Springfield, VA 22152-2456, info@practicalparrot.com.

Illustrations: Bill Crowley of Colorado Smiles and Katherine Skaggs
Cover & Interior Design: IRIE Publishing & Productions

ISBN 0-9678820-0-1

Printed in Canada by Hignell Book Printing.

CONTENTS

ACKNOWLEDGEMENTS

- To Cindy Kessler and "Herman" for their enthusiastic testing of our designs and ideas and providing invaluable feedback.

- To all our feathered companions for being such beautiful, playful, and patient creatures and providing the inspiration for this book.

- To Irene Pepperberg who lent us her laptop on that day in October when we announced we were going to write a book and said, "go for it!"

- To Donna Murphy of IRIE Publishing & Productions for helping us believe we could do this and showing us the way.

- To Deb of SuperBird Toys for giving so generously of her time and talent.

- To all our supportive friends and family members for sharing in our excitement.

PREFACE

I'll never forget it. Baby, my Umbrella Cockatoo was about six months old and we were playing on the floor. During the course of our frolicking, he ran over and took a chunk out of a nearby baseboard. I can still recall my amazement. It was so effortless—so "parrot-like." "How cute!" I remember saying, delighting in the discoveries of a new bird owner. Now eight years later I can still find woodwork, furniture, and even clothes that bear testament to that mischievous and powerful beak.

Keeping beaks busy and avian minds occupied is an ongoing challenge for all companion bird owners. We want the best for our incredible feathered friends. We want them to be happily occupied. We want them to have fun.

It is estimated that about sixty million parrots are kept as pets in the U.S. Sadly, many of them don't stay in the same home for more than a few years. Whether hatched in Seattle or South America, they are still wild animals. With this 'wildness' comes some very specific needs. To remain physically and psychologically healthy, parrots must be allowed to chew, to spend time with their flock (you), to work at finding food, and to solve problems and figure things out.

This is why toys and away-from-the-cage play areas are so important to the well-being of a parrot. These items are not "extras" in the life of a bird—they are necessities. Parrot toys engage beaks, minds, and bodies in activities comparable to those done in natural surroundings. Play areas located away from the cage provide a parrot-safe location for family (flock) interaction. To remain healthy and happy, our parrots need to play.

Providing for "birdie Buzz Saws" and "avian Einsteins" can be a daunting task! All of us pet bird owners are forever on the lookout for new play ideas—whether it's something we can buy or make ourselves. That's what this book is all about.

Both long-time and new parrot owners will find practical advice, safety tips, and loads of ideas for toys and play areas that can be bought or made. This book includes suggestions for quick, around-the-house toys and plans for complicated play area projects. It can be read over and over. There will always be something new to try. We had a lot of fun writing this book (and so did our birds!). It was an exciting project. We hope you will find it exciting too. So find your feathered friend and get ready to have some fun!

FOREWORD

In the past three decades, parrots have gone from being primarily exotic creatures seen in zoos to being among the more popular of pets. Unlike cats and dogs, however, parrots (except maybe for budgerigars and cockatiels) have not been domesticated—the typical bird that is purchased is at most three generations removed from the forest, savanna, or jungle of origin. Thus it is still a wild creature with all of its natural behavior patterns intact. We can tame these birds and thereby teach them to be acceptable members of our family, but by doing so we are asking them to learn the rules of a completely alien "flock." Can we use our knowledge of their ancestry—the skills that allow the wild parrot to forage, build and defend a nest, keep in optimal physical tone, attract and guard a mate, raise its young—to mediate this process? Such is the premise of this book, the first of a series, by D'Arezzo and Nunn. In this volume, the authors help readers to understand the physical and mental needs of their birds and how to decide upon the toys and play areas that will meet these needs as well as those of the owners' lifestyles. This book clearly fills an important niche for any current parrot owner and will help prospective parrot owners know what to expect of their feathered companions—a difficult job, done with wit and humor.

— Irene Pepperberg, PhD
Associate Professor of Ecology and Evolutionary Biology,
University of Arizona
Visiting Associate Professor, The Media Lab, MIT

PART 1

Parrot Toys: The Ticket to Fun

SALE AT THE
PARROT EMPORIUM

A LITTLE STORY...

"Look at this crowd! I hope there's some good things left by the time we get in." Baby the Umbrella Cockatoo said to her friend Pebbles the slender-billed conure.

"Listen to all the screaming in there. You know how it is when a bunch of parrots get together for a toy sale!" exclaimed Pebbles.

Even though Baby and Pebbles love to go toy shopping together, their tastes run in different directions. Baby loves a toy she can sink her large powerful beak into. Pebbles, on the other hand, has a long slender curved beak. Chewing doesn't turn her on. She finds it rather brutish. Pebbles would rather admire the hues of multicolored cloth as she weaves them through her cage bars.

"What to chew? What to chew?" Baby mused to herself as she perused the wall of brightly colored wooden toys. "Did you find anything yet, Pebbles?"

Pebbles popped her head up through a pile of cloth and leather toys. "I think I've found something to keep me busy for awhile. Look at this delightful combination of cloth, leather, and jute strands!"

"That's fine for you artsy types. Me, I think I'll go with this three-foot long wooden Chew-a-Rama!" shouted Baby over the mayhem. "Shall we pick out something for your friend PJ the male Eclectus while we're here?"

"I have just the thing. It's hard plastic and he can slide these beads along the rods. You know he likes to manipulate things," Pebble replies. "Like you," winked Baby, "I know we could make a lot of these toys ourselves, but it's so much fun to go shopping!"

1 WHAT ARE WE GOING TO CHEW TODAY?

Providing projects that occupy busy beaks and stimulate avian Einsteins is one of the never-ending challenges of parrot ownership. The quest for that perfect bird toy takes us trekking to innumerable pet shops and bird marts and poring through countless catalogs.

Keeping our feathered dynamo busy is indeed a top priority for companion bird owners. This is no easy task with a creature that boasts the intelligence of a human toddler with an attention span to match!

Whether he's hanging out on a playstand with the "flock" or spending some quality time alone in his cage, your feathered friend needs to have something to do.

2 JUNGLE JOBS

Everyone knows that parrots should have "toys." It has been documented that just about every intelligent creature delights in "playing." For your feathered companion who is only a generation or two away from his wild cousins in the jungle, this "playing" takes on a whole different meaning. It might not be as much "playing" as it is "working." Just as we get up in the morning and have a *job* to go to, so it is with wild parrots.

In their natural habitat, parrots lead busy and active lives. Noisy flocks leave roosting areas in the morning often flying for miles to begin foraging for breakfast. Feeding activities may involve scouring the ground for seeds or performing a highwire act in the jungle canopy to go after succulent fruits. A scarlet macaw with its powerful beak might work diligently to dislodge a tasty kernel from a leather-like pod. In another part of the world, a cockatoo may rip open a rotting tree trunk looking for tasty grubs. The search for food demands a lot of energy and dexterity every day.

But it's not all work in the jungle. Parrots in the wild spend a considerable amount of time honing and cleaning their beaks. By biting and chewing on hard objects, they keep their beaks in good condition and exercise their powerful facial muscles. An afternoon rainstorm may bring some birds out to hang upside down from branches and scream in delight as water soaks their feathers. And being inquisitive and intelligent creatures, parrots engage in some activities just for *fun*. Cockatoos have been seen stripping bark and leaves from branches as they sit whiling away the afternoon hours.

3 NOT JUST A TOY, BUT A PARROT TOY!

We're too intelligent to just hang out in our cage all day with nothing to do.

Without the jungle to play, work, and forage in, your bird will need some awesome substitutions! Therefore, toys have a large role to play in the well-being of your companion parrot. That feathered dynamo in your living room is still "genetically programmed" with the same needs of its wild cousins.

A parrot that spends his days locked in his cage with little to occupy his beak or mind is being deprived of the stimulation that he needs to stay psychologically healthy. Being reluctant to buy a parrot a toy because "all he'll do is chew it up" is to ignore the needs of these incredible companions.

Toys for parrots are not really *playthings* or *rewards*—rather, they are **necessities**. They provide the essential activities that these inquisitive and intelligent creatures must engage in to stay physically and mentally healthy. Because many people tend to associate the word *toy* with something frivolous, from now on we will use the term **parrot toy** to refer to this very important object.

A **parrot toy** is an object that provides opportunities for **natural** activities similar to those that would occur in the wild. A **parrot toy** can be designed to be mentally or physically challenging, to teach, or to entertain. Again, a toy is not an option but a necessity! Although we will often use the words *fun* and *play*, we are really referring to a very **essential** activity for your parrot.

4 WHAT PIG?

One of the reasons some pet parrots don't have enough useable parrot toys in their cages (or in some cases, *any* parrot toys at all) is because it's awfully hard to fork over hard earned cash to have the new purchase literally disappear overnight.

Baby the Umbrella Cockatoo—one of the "characters" in the little story that began this chapter—is in real life quite a voracious chewer. One of his most memorable "parrot-toy events" occurred one morning when he was given a large wooden pink pig on a chain. The pig was at least one-inch thick. It had a large red wooden apple hanging from a hole in its middle and a variety of tempting wooden blocks and such dangling from its body.

Pink Pig set Carol back somewhere around $35 to $40 but she figured it was worth it because it certainly had lots of *chew* potential. Imagine Carol's surprise when she returned home from work that afternoon to find nothing left but a red wooden apple swinging from a chain. The wooden splinters were piled so high in the bottom of Baby's cage that they came up over the bottom grate!

But we can't deny them their parrot toys. We just have to **buy smart, re-use, re-assemble,** and be **creative** with the inexpensive and the free. And that's what the rest of this chapter is all about!

A parrot with nothing to do is a prime candidate for behavioral problems. A bird in a cage filled with stimulating things to explore will usually be more interested in chewing a new colorful array of wooden blocks than screaming. Shredding a "feather duster" might prove to be more satisfying than shredding a feather. **Set yourself up for success.** Plenty of parrot toys can help prevent some problems before they start.

5 YIKES! WHAT'S THAT?

Be sensitive to your bird when introducing new parrot toys. Parrots are prey animals in the wild (meaning that if they're not careful they could end up as something's lunch!), so they are "programmed" to be naturally cautious and suspicious of new things. Some birds will tolerate new toys without much ado—others may be quite fearful.

One technique that works well is to place the toy **outside** the cage but within eyesight for a few days, moving it closer every day. Placing it on the floor or a nearby table works well. Toys may also be hung on the outside of the cage **(lower** than the bird's perch), gradually raised up, and eventually put inside the cage. When hanging a new parrot toy inside the cage, try not to place it too close to food or the water bowl at first. If your bird is fearful, it may prevent him from approaching his bowls. Holding the toy near your face and playing with it within eyesight of your bird helps to show that this new object is "ok."

As a rule of a thumb, avoid introducing new things near bedtime. Imagine how you would feel if the lights were turned off and here was this strange, scary new thing in your bedroom!

For young birds or phobic birds, purchasing parrot toys one size smaller than the recommended size can make toy introduction easier. If you have more than one parrot, giving the toy to a nonphobic bird to play with first allows the more cautious bird to see that it is *safe*. Never force a parrot toy onto a frightened parrot. Take your time, be patient, and you will end up with a bird that enjoys his toys and trusts you.

Be sensitive when providing swings for young parrots whose sense of balance and dexterity is not yet fully developed. They are often quite klutzy! Hanging a swing very low in the cage can prevent a frightening fall. Gradually raise it as your bird matures and becomes more adept. Parrots with newly trimmed nails or wings can also be clumsier than normal.

6 JUST GIVE ME A LITTLE TIME HERE...

You've just spent $24.99 on a new, store-bought parrot toy *or* you've just spent 30 precious minutes putting together a great homemade parrot toy. You put it in your parrot's cage and he could care less. "Look! Look! Look at your new toy!" All you get is a blank stare in return. What to do? In a word—nothing. Remember that this is a cautious creature. It will take him some time to warm up to his new plaything. First, be sure you have hung the parrot toy where your buddy can reach it. Near

a perch is usually a good place to start. Give him a week or two. If after that time it's still untouched, then move it someplace else in the cage.

Sometimes removing a parrot toy and reintroducing it later helps. Some parrots, because of years of deprivation may not know how to *play* with parrot toys. Sometimes watching you having a great time with a new parrot toy will help to get the message across.

Also watching a *model* such as another bird in the flock who enjoys his toys will help teach the hesitant parrot what parrot toys are all about. Be patient. Proceed slowly. Eventually a parrot's exploratory nature will win over.

7 MY PARROT'S GOT STYLE!

If you asked any four people what they enjoy doing for fun, you would probably get four different answers. One may enjoy gardening, while another takes to the links. A third delights in a good book, while the last may find skydiving to be the ultimate way to recreate. Parrots are no different. Not every bird *plays* the same way. You might say that parrots have different **play styles**. Species, personality, and background determine a bird's play style.

Knowing your feathered friend's play style will help you choose parrot toys and activities especially for him. Take a look at the play styles described below and have some fun trying to figure out what your bird likes to do for entertainment. Your parrot will undoubtedly fit into several categories. His play style may even change depending on his age and the time of the year.

There are two main groups:

High Energy—These are parrots that are always on the move—all you see is a blur of feathers. They may or may not be heavy chewers. They tend to be rambunctious and sometimes mischievous. With flapping wings and indignant squawks, they like to do battle with their parrot toys. In their exuberance, they may fall off their perches and gyms. Swings, mobiles, and noisemakers appeal to these guys. Amazons, macaws, and cockatoos will often exhibit this type of play style.

Low Energy—These parrots are quieter and somewhat more sedate. They tend to be more detail oriented. While some Low Energy players are heavy chewers, many are not. They tend to prefer parrot toys hung close to their face. They often delight in things to preen and weave, puzzles, and softer chew toys. Eclectus, African Greys, and Poicephalus are often Low Energy players.

Besides the two categories above, there are other play style variations:

- **Manipulators**—This group loves to take things apart. Not only do they delight in disassembling their parrot toys, but also their cages and gyms as well. They can be accomplished escape artists. Manipulators get a big kick out of unscrewing the quick link that holds the parrot toy and watching it fall to the floor of the cage. Keep these guys busy with puzzles—the more intricate the better.

- **Buzz Saws**—These parrots need wood and plenty of it! They are very beak oriented and need a constant supply of things to chew. If parrot toys are scarce, they will often start destroying their perches. Keeping them in "chewables" can be a continual challenge. Consider alternatives to wood, for example corrugated boxes.

- **Weavers**—These are the artistic types. They can spend hours weaving things in and out of plastic chain links or through the cage bars. They like to stuff things— sometimes food—into tiny holes in other parrot toys. Strands of raffia, ribbon, leather, or jute can provide endless fun for weaving and preening.

- **Gatherers**—This group is into collectibles. Favorite things such as toys, bits of toys, and even food can find its way into a Gatherer's cache. Oscar, Carol's Quaker, stashes his goodies in a pile on top of his cage while Baby the Umbrella prefers hiding his tidbits in a box at the bottom of the cage. Small , foot-sized parrot toys and wood pieces can be a Gatherer's delight.

- **Acrobats**—These birds would just as soon hang by a toenail than stand on two feet. They are as much at home walking upside down in their cage as right side up. A 360-degree turn around a perch? No problem! Acrobats can also be found lying on their backs or even standing on their heads. Swings, hanging ropes, and spiral perches are a must for these guys.

- **Hide and Seekers**—Parrots in this category seem to always be peering out at you from their secret spot. Sometimes they're shy; sometimes they just like their own private hideaway. Huts and tubes are fun for the Hide and Seekers. Parrot toys themselves can be lined up along a perch and used as a shield for those who like their privacy.

- **Companions**—These guys are looking for parrot toys to be fellow cage-mates rather than something to chew on or destroy. While these birds rarely destroy their toys, they may bump into them to get them moving or snuggle next to them. Owners of Companions often lament that their birds "don't play with toys." These parrots probably have the subtlest **play style** of all.

No two parrots play alike as Carol's four blue and gold macaws so aptly illustrate.

Bubba is a High Energy/Buzz Saw. His favorite chewable is a large cardboard box.

Chaco is a Low Energy/Buzz Saw/Hide and Seeker. He sits in one spot, loves to chew, but needs his privacy.

Zac is a Low Energy/semi-Buzz Saw/Manipulator. Missing two toes on one foot makes it a little harder for him to get around. However, he is a gifted escape artist.

Finally, Ali is a High Energy/Manipulator/Acrobat. And quite a handful!

Although we have emphasized the larger parrots in this section, don't forget the little ones. There are plenty of Buzz Saw cockatiels and Acrobatic lovebirds out there too!

8 LET'S TALK ABOUT INTERIOR DECORATING

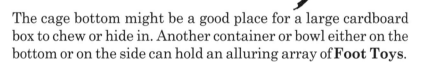

Parrot owners often lament that their birds don't utilize all or even much of their cage. One way to entice your feathered friend to explore his surroundings is to set his cage up with *projects* at multiple levels. Parrot toys provide the projects.

The cage bottom might be a good place for a large cardboard box to chew or hide in. Another container or bowl either on the bottom or on the side can hold an alluring array of **Foot Toys**.

Parrot toys in the middle level can be accessible from perches and swings. If you have a bird that enjoys cruising upside down on the top of his cage, hang a toy there. Don't forget parrot toys that fit onto the perches themselves for something a little different. Parrot toys that attach to the sides of the cage such as busy boards and abacus-type toys can work at any level.

Large parrot toys, particularly those made with thin slices of tree trunk, can actually form new levels within the cage for playing. Baby the Umbrella has several *levels* of tree trunk slices on which he likes to store wood chips for further chewing. His cage is always *messy* with toy bits and pieces, and he has things to play with in every nook and cranny. Carol encourages this and, except for soiled items, avoids removing most of his *treasures*.

Special-needs parrots present another challenge. Birds with missing or damaged toes or feet may need thicker perches to feel comfortable. Perches may also be wrapped with jute, cohesive flexible bandage such as Vetrap®, or leather. Utilize the sides of the cages particularly near a preferred perch for hanging parrot toys. Paco, Lauren's one-footed Amazon, enjoys a busy board attached near his favorite leather perch. Libby, Carol's blind Timneh, has all her parrot toys lined up behind her upper perch. She can work her way down the perch feeling for new items.

For shy or frightened parrots, consider hanging several parrot toys as a "shield" in front of a high corner perch, for example.

All birds benefit from a place in their cage where they can be somewhat "out of sight." In the wild, despite their brilliant coloration, parrots can become almost invisible when hiding among the leaves and shadows.

Sitting exposed in an empty cage can be very stressful for a creature whose survival depends on being able to blend into its surroundings. Use your parrot toys to create a miniature jungle where there are places to play and places to hide. Remember to think *levels* in a cage and give your buddy something fun to do wherever he may roam in his cage!

9 'ROUND AND 'ROUND WE GO

Rotating your parrot toys is an excellent habit to get into. Every month or so, replace one or two parrot toys either with new toys, or *old* new toys found in your bird's toy chest.

This keeps things interesting for you and your feathered companion. By doing this, all parrot toys become *new* toys over and over. One exception to the rotation rule might be your bird's *favorite* parrot toy. Consider leaving it in the cage—just where it is. If it gets destroyed, buy or make him a new one.

Removing parrot toys from the cage to recycle is a good time to clean them, cut frayed rope, and do general maintenance. This will increase the life of the toy and keep them safe for your bird. Remember that cleaning and safety checks should be done frequently to all parrot toys inside the cage as well.

Often when a used parrot toy has been hanging in the cage for awhile the remaining pieces of wood are too big for your pal to chew. When rotating your parrot toys consider taking these toys apart, cutting the wooden parts into smaller pieces, and using them for some homemade toys.

Large wooden balls and tubes can be sawed into smaller sections and restrung. Chunks of wood placed in a "toy bowl" can become crunchable **Foot Toys**. Small parrots often delight in the leavings from the large parrots. Toothpicks from a macaw's chew-fest can keep a Quaker happy for days!

10 ALWAYS PLAY IT SAFE!

Before you rush out to buy or make your feathered friend some parrot toys, read the **IMPORTANT** parrot toy maintenance and safety list below. As a caring and conscientious parrot owner, always keep the following points in mind:

- **No parrot toy is 100% safe**. Monitor your bird with every **new** toy. The more *active* your parrot, the greater the chance your bird could get himself into a potentially dangerous situation. Never give a bird a new parrot toy and then leave for the day.

- **Old**, well-loved parrot toys can pose a hazard for your bird. Watch for frayed cotton rope or long strands of any material. These can be treacherous for a parrot. Birds have been known to get cotton rope wrapped around their toes, necks, and wings. "Frankie," a one-legged lovebird given to the Gabriel Foundation—a rescue and rehabilitative organization in Aspen, Colorado—was a victim of such an unfortunate mishap. He had gotten a small piece of thread wrapped around his toe one evening. By the next morning his foot was dead. It took three amputations and the loss of his leg to save his life. No need to be overly suspicious of every toy—just be careful.

- Keep toys **clean** and free from droppings and other debris. Most things can go into the dishwasher. Leather, rawhide, and wood contaminated with droppings should be discarded. These are organic products and it is virtually impossible to thoroughly clean them.

- Pick the right parrot toy for your bird's **size** and **strength**. Read the toy label for recommendations, but also know your bird and how he plays.

- Hang parrot toys using only the following **parrot-safe methods**:

– **Leather**—Use only untanned or vegetable tanned leather. If you can't find this at a craft store, you can order it from some parrot toy catalogs. Conventionally tanned leather contains uric acid and formaldehyde. Avoid the use of leather shoelaces for this reason.

– **Sisal, jute, hemp, or cotton rope** (no nylon)—This is best purchased from a craft store. Some sisal may be treated with creosote or other chemicals. Buy the proper diameter for your size bird.

– **Closed-link chain** only (such as found in dog choke collars)—no jack chain or double-looped chain. See the note about zinc below.

– **Quick links**—Avoid the use of dog lead clips, carabiners, or any spring-loaded type clip. Also avoid round key rings. These can trap heads, toes, beaks, or tongues. See the notes about zinc below.

– **Plastic cable ties**—These are an inexpensive way to attach parrot toys to the cage. Some birds can chew through them so they may not be appropriate for everyone. Be sure to pull these tight. **Plastic chain** (the kind sold for parrots) or the **open plastic links** sold for baby toys can also be used.

A BRIEF WORD ABOUT ZINC

Zinc—Unless it specifies stainless steel, most of the chain and quick links available on parrot toys and in hardware stores are coated with zinc, which is a potentially poisonous heavy metal. If you have a parrot that spends a lot of time playing with quick links or chain in his mouth, you might want to consider buying stainless steel hardware.

Many birds, however, do not *chew* the hardware to any great degree. If you have any concerns about your parrot ingesting zinc, then switch to stainless steel.

- Remove any **loops** of chain, leather, or rope which can become a noose to trap necks or wings. Any rings used in parrot toys should be large enough in diameter so that your bird can pass his body through and not become wedged.

- **Avoid!** Jingle bells (can trap toes and beaks) and costume jewelry (dangerous metals, small parts, and potential for entrapment). Keep strands (jute, sisal, cotton rope, chain) **short!** One to four inches depending on the size of the bird is appropriate. If fabric is used in a parrot toy, always remove any loose threads that can become wrapped around toes.

11 IT'S PLAYTIME

Open a catalog or go to the bird store and you will see an explosion of brightly colored wood, mirrors, and acrylic. They might be strung together with ropes, chain, leather, or cloth. Some are as tiny as your thumb and others weigh 20 pounds and are almost as tall as you! Overwhelming? You bet! Where do you start? Which are the perfect parrot toys for your feathered buddy?

What to buy? What's the best toy?

To put some order into this bewildering array and to aid you in making informed decisions about what to buy or make your bird, we have divided the multitude of parrot toys into **Eleven Parrot-Toy Categories.** Just about every parrot toy out there will fit into one of these categories. Needless to say, these are not hard-and-fast groupings and there will be some overlap. That's ok. The idea is to furnish guidelines to assist you in providing the widest possible range of activities for your bird.

In describing each category, we mention the **natural** parrot activity this parrot toy might duplicate. Under each category we also give you ideas for low- or no-cost parrot toys that can keep your companion happy for just pennies a day (**Cheep! Cheep!**).

For maximum skill building and enjoyment, outfit your buddy's cage with a parrot toy from at least *four* of the Parrot-Toy Categories. This variety will give your bird a chance to use all his parrot skills. You may find that he prefers some varieties and has no interest in others. That's fine. But every now and then, try a new category and put some spice in his life!

Are you ready to get your feathered friend chewing, swinging, puzzling, and cuddling? It's time to explore the Eleven Parrot-Toy Categories!

Cuddlers

In the wild, most parrots like to be in physical contact with their mate, clutchmate, parents, or friends while roosting.

I just love to cuddle my soft toys!

FOR EXAMPLE...

Cuddlers can be soft, furry pieces of material attached to the side of the cage to cuddle and sleep against. Included in this category are also little "huts" or tubes in which to hide and sleep. A Cuddler can be a perfect hide away for a shy parrot. Huts may not be appropriate for some parrots during mating season as they may get a little too territorial about their favorite spot. Sometimes well used parrot toys with puffs of cotton rope become Cuddlers when a parrot gets in the habit of snuggling next to the soft rope.

Always monitor your parrot to be sure they are not ingesting any stuffing of furry material in a Cuddler. One sign that may indicate that your bird is ingesting the material is the presence of shredded cotton at the bottom of the cage. If you see this, remove the parrot toy immediately.

CHEEP! CHEEP!

- Stuffed animals from the thrift store (wash and remove eyes, etc.) are easy to find Cuddlers. Be sure to buy the ones that are filled with fiber and not beads or beans. These can be attached with cable ties to the side of the cage near a favorite perch.

- Hand-sewn pillows, huts, or tubes.

- A clean, empty orange juice can hung in a cage can be a great hideaway for a cockatiel, parakeet, or lovebird.

- *Coconut Hideaway*—This little hideaway/swing is perfect for any of the little guys. You will need half of a coconut, cleaned with the meat removed. Drill four holes equally spaced along the rim. Run a leather strip at least 10 inches long into each hole. Knot each end. Draw the four strips together above the coconut and knot. Hang in the cage.

Noisemakers

To impress a potential mate, a male Palm Cockatoo will beat a hollow log with a stick. Parrots have also been observed screaming into hollow logs and drumming with their beaks. Parrots love noise!

FOR EXAMPLE...

Noisemakers are any parrot toy that rings, rattles, dings, or clatters. A Noisemaker can be as simple as a bell or as complicated as a parrot music box. Bells are probably the most popular and can be hung alone or attached to just about any other parrot toy. Also included in this category are sections of bamboo with wooden balls held by chains that clatter against the outside of the cylinder.

Besides just banging a bell around, parrots often use bells to "make a statement" and even show emotion. Lauren's slender-billed conure, Pebbles, and Carol's African Gray, Murray, both use bells to say such things as, "Hey, look at me!" and "Come back!" Murray has bells everywhere in his cage so that whenever the moment seizes him, he is ready to jangle.

Cockatiels often love to sit with their a bell on their head. One potential problem with bells is that parrots can sometimes pull the clappers out. Be sure any bell on a parrot toy is appropriate for the strength of your bird. If you are unsure, replace the bell or simply remove the clapper with needlenose pliers. Copper and stainless steel bells are the safest.

CHEEP! CHEEP!

- Hang a bell by itself using a parrot-safe method or add one to any regular parrot toy.

- *Dixie Ding-Dong*—A flat wooden ice cream spoon hung inside an inverted dixie cup makes a simple "bell" for a smaller parrot.

- *Flowerpot Bell*—An inverted plastic flowerpot with a "clapper" inside makes an unusual bell. The clapper can be a marbella bead, a bell, or a wooden block. Attach the clapper to parrot-safe chain or leather and run it up through the hole in the bottom of the pot. A knot in the leather or a quick link in the chain will hold it in place under the pot. Eclectus in particular are fond of sitting with their heads up under their "bell."

- *King Kong Bell*—For a large parrot such as a Hyacinth macaw, try a stainless steel bucket with a "clapper" made of a stainless steel restaurant serving spoon. Drill a hole in the bottom of the bucket being sure that there are no exposed sharp edges. Use parrot-safe chain as above to hang the clapper and bucket.

Puzzlers

All parrots are by nature inquisitive and curious creatures.

FOR EXAMPLE...

Puzzlers are parrot toys that require a parrot to solve a problem. The reward may be food, smaller toy pieces, or the undoing of the toy itself. Some examples of Puzzlers are: acrylic holders that dispense or hide popsicle sticks or treats, a bell inside an acrylic tube, or a metal box held together with wingnuts and bolts. Another Puzzler on the market consists of a metal "basket" with a removable lid into which paper, wood, and other treasurers can be stuffed and then pulled out through the openings. When filled with dried fruit or nuts it becomes a **Food Finder**. Puzzlers may also be parrot toys that require some degree of manipulation to move beads or marbles in acrylic tubes. Puzzlers can keep your feathered friend occupied for hours!

Ali Macaw, one of Carol's macaws, turns every parrot toy into a Puzzler. She was given a metal canister with a screw-on lid that held a few treats. The object was to unscrew the lid and eventually retrieve the treat. The canister was bolted onto a bracket and the bracket was bolted onto the cage. After about 20 minutes, Carol decided to see how "Ali" was getting along with her latest challenge ("This should keep her busy for hours!"). In 20 minutes, not only had she managed to get the treat out of the canister, but also the canister off the bracket and the bracket off the cage ("Anything else you want me to take apart?").

 **CHEEP! CHEEP!**

- *Glove or Sock Surprise*—Fill a clean, light colored sock or all-cotton work glove with plastic beads, bits of wood, short pieces of rope with knots, cork, twigs, dog biscuits, scrunched paper, nuts, etc. Tie shut at the top with jute or leather and hang from cage.

- *What's in the Box?*—For this you will need a clean cardboard box of an appropriate size for your parrot. Let your parrot watch you fill the box with goodies— rattle it a few times, put it in the cage and watch the fun. These may be hung in the cage or simply placed on the cage bottom.

- *Knots to You*—Put single, double, and triple knots in leather, sisal, or cotton rope. Attach to the cage and let your parrot undo.

- *Bolt Board*—Cut a piece of ½-inch board suitable for your bird. Drill a row of holes that will accommodate the size of bolt you will be using. Use one of the holes to hang the wood in the cage. Use stainless steel nuts, bolts, and washers. Arrange them so that nuts appear on both sides of the board.

- *Rawhide Taco*—Boil water. Drop in a flat round piece of rawhide ("flips") and let soften. Remove. Lay lengths of wood, twigs, popsicle sticks, craft sticks, knotted strands of jute, etc. down the middle of the "taco." They should be long enough so that they hang over the side. Fold up like a taco. Put holes in the top with an awl. Run a small piece of leather through the holes. Let dry and harden. Hang in cage.

Destructibles

In the jungle, parrots engage in such activities as chiseling at nest holes and tearing up branches looking for food.

FOR EXAMPLE...

Destructibles are parrots toys that are primarily made of wood, rawhide, or any other chewable material that can be destroyed. Destructibles are important parrot toys. All parrots, from little budgies to Hyacinth macaws must have access to chewable wood. Making toothpicks is critical to the psychological well-being of our feathered friends. Even Libby, Carol's blind Timneh African Grey, does an admirable job of chewing up her Destructible parrot toys. Because wooden parrot toys are meant to be destroyed, it is important to note that wood varies in its *crunch potential*. Some woods are harder than others to chew. Pieces of manzanita, bamboo, and arbutus are appropriate for larger birds. They are pretty tough for smaller birds to destroy. For the little guys, or birds that aren't big chewers, buy toys with smaller pieces of softer wood such as pine or cholla. Be aware of the fact that some parrots tend to be more destructive during certain times of the year—usually during the breeding period. Non-chewers may begin to chew, and heavy-duty chewers may turn into Buzz Saws. Be sure to have plenty of Destructibles on hand.

 **CHEEP! CHEEP!**

- Items found around the house that are fun to destroy (rather than the new dining room set) are: cardboard, cereal or cracker boxes, oatmeal boxes, phone books/ pages, paper towel rolls (left long or cut into rings), clean unused corks, scrap paper, junk mail (no staples or plastic windows), cardboard egg cartons (that did not contain any broken eggs), a box of white tissues, clean palm leaves (these can be woven together). The favorite parrot toy of Bubba, one of Carol's Blue and Gold macaws, is a corrugated box, the bigger the better. He will spend hours at the bottom of his cage demolish his box.

- A Destructible can be as simple as a thick piece of corrugated cardboard hung in the cage.

- Dried field corn (the kind you feed to squirrels) can be an entertaining Destructible parrot toy. Be sure it contains no mold. A screweye on a parrot-safe chain screwed into one end is an easy way to hang the corn in your bird's cage.

- Pinecones make great Destructibles either hung in the cage or as a **Foot Toy**. Follow the guidelines for the gathering of safe woods as outlined below. Pinecones can be sterilized by baking in a 225-degree oven for 20 minutes.

- Natural blond willow wreaths, both circular and heart-shaped, are inexpensive Destructible parrot toys that may be purchased at a craft shop. They come in various sizes to suit any parrot. Even parakeets enjoy making matchsticks out of these. For added interest, tie bits of brightly colored cloth, beads, and small wooden pieces to the wreath. On some of the larger ones, try stuffing small nuts such as pistachios among the willow branches for a Food Finder.

- An entire roll of unscented white toweling or toilet paper makes an interesting Destructible. If you don't want it to unravel, tie a piece of jute tightly around the roll. Attach a "stopper" made out of a wooden blck, or something similar, on one end of a chain, run up through the roll, and hang in the cage. Lauren's slender-billed conure "Pebbles" loves to weave the toilet paper hanging in her cage through the cage bars to the point where Lauren says it looks as if someone came and "TP'd" her cage.

- *Food Chews*—Food can become a Destructible parrot toy that is fun as well as nutritious. Try whole carrots complete with the green tops, broccoli stalks, large leaves of greens such as chard and kale, whole oranges, ears of corn, pomegranates, and pumpkin halves with seeds. Food items can be wedged between cage bars, clipped into place, or cable tied. A food skewer, available just about everywhere that sells parrot toys, is another method of hanging your yummy Destructibles. (The skewers can also be strung with small wooden shapes for a "refillable" wooden parrot toy.) Sections of sugarcane may be purchased at most grocery stores. Screw a screweye into one end and hang with a chain or leather.

- *Go Natural*—Branches gathered from trees provide free, easily obtainable Destructible parrot toys. A parrot can spend an entire afternoon stripping bark from branches. Follow these guidelines when collecting wood to ensure that it is parrot safe:

1 – Do not collect wood that has been sprayed with pesticides, chemicals, or is exposed to exhaust fumes. Be sure it is free from insects, rot, and mold.

2 – As a general rule of thumb, if you are not positive it is safe, don't give it to your bird.

3 – Wood can be sterilized by baking in a 250-degree oven for 1½ hours.

4 – Branches can also be scrubbed with a nontoxic disinfectant such as a 10-percent bleach solution, rinsed well and allowed to dry.

Below is a list of some parrot-safe wood that is suitable for perches and chewing:

- Safe wood: ash, arbutus, bamboo, beech, birch, crabapple, dogwood, fir, grapevine, pine, magnolia, manzanita, spruce, willow.

- Other sources of wood that can be used *as is* or strung together to make some unique Destructible parrot toys are: wooden baby toys (e.g., blocks, beads, etc.), wooden kitchen utensils, unstenciled paint stirrers, scrap lumber (be sure it is not pressure treated), small wooden craft pieces such as balls, spools, etc. (many of these have predrilled holes), wireless clothespins, popsicle and craft sticks, and prepackaged colored wood sold as pet rodent chews. Some parrot toy catalogs also sell replacement toy-making parts.

- *Get Colorful*—If you want to get really fancy you can color your wood or rawhide by using one of the methods below:

  1 – Unsweetened Kool Aid™, food coloring, or Easter egg coloring kits work well for adding color to homemade wooden parrot toys.

• Toy pieces can be soaked in one package of Kool Aid™ to 1 cup of hot water. This produces soft pastel colors and is great for wooden shapes found at the craft store.

• Food coloring can be diluted with a very small amount of water or used straight.

• The use of sweet substances such as Jello™ is discouraged because of the risk that birds will ingest the "flavored" wood. If there is a danger that your parrot will ingest *anything* with a flavor, avoid the use of Kool Aid™ also and use only food coloring. Always monitor your companion parrot with colored wood parrot toys for this reason.

2 – Confectionary coloring paste found in bakery supply stores produces bolder colors. Paint this on the wood-like paint.

3 – Tempera or other paints that are nontoxic and made for children are parrot-safe. These can be found in craft stores, toy stores, and sometimes grocery stores. These too may be painted directly on the wood.

• If you use glue in a parrot toy, use nontoxic, child-safe Elmer's™ glue.

• Save chain, leather, quick links, beads, and rings from store-bought parrot toys. These can be strung with new wood pieces as mentioned above, and presto! —a new parrot toy!

• When using leather or rope to string parrot toys, always put a knot in between each wooden piece. This way if your feathered buddy unties the bottom knot all the pieces won't slide off! When stringing wooden pieces on chain, you can use a "pear" link (for smaller parrots) or a **small** piece of cotton rope through the end of the chain to keep everything in place.

With the hints we've given you, get out your food coloring and drill and let your imagination run wild. Your parrot will thank you!

Nondestructibles

In the wild, parrots use hard substances to hone and clean their beaks.

FOR EXAMPLE...

Nondestructibles are generally parrot toys made of acrylic, PVC, rawhide, plastic, or heavy nylon. Many of these parrot toys are usually dishwasher safe. Nondestructibles are often brightly colored and fashioned into mobiles or puzzles. Some examples are acrylic mobiles with dice or keys hanging from them, mirror cubes, dangling men figures, and marbella bead and plastic ring or chain toys. Because some folks don't understand the need for parrots to chew and destroy their toys, they fill their cage with Nondestructible parrot toys. As you can see this is only *one* category of the eleven that we have listed and your pet should have the opportunity to sample parrot toys from *all* the categories. However, for the parrot that is prone to *ingesting* his toys, these may be the only safe alternative.

CHEEP! CHEEP!

- Human baby toys such as plastic keys, nesting cups, and other heavy-duty plastic children's toys available from the thrift, toy, or grocery store can make appropriate inexpensive parrot toys. Chains can formed from plastic links used to attach baby toys to strollers and high chairs.

- It is possible to buy scrap acrylic pieces by the pound from an acrylic manufacturer. Acrylic tubes and blocks are often available too. These are brightly colored and easy to drill through. Use a scroll or chop saw to cut shapes such as hearts, squares, circles, etc. They can be strung in a mobile form or in various designs. **Warning**—fumes are released from the cutting and drilling of acrylics, so do this away from your parrot.

- Large pieces of rawhide are virtually indestructible for most parrots. If you want to get fancy and color them, follow the guidelines for safe coloring found under Destructible parrot toys. Check the rawhide when purchasing to confirm that it is made in the U.S. Rawhide processed in other countries often contains formaldehyde.

- Knot the end of a strand of leather then string on beads, big buttons, bells, plastic rings and hang in cage. This can be fun for the smaller birds such as cockatiels and lovebirds.

- Keys and metal or plastic measuring spoons hung with leather or a cable tie can be a simple Nondestructible.

Food Finders

In their natural habitat, this activity occupies most of a parrot's day!

FOR EXAMPLE...

Food Finders are any parrot toy that requires your bird to *work* for his food. These parrot toys may be PVC peanut holders; acrylic, leather, or coconut treat hiders; nuts imbedded in wood or special clay; and food skewers to make kabobs. If you use foods other than nuts, dried fruits or seeds, remember to remove the treat before it spoils, in case your bird hasn't already done that for you.

As we mentioned earlier, our Eleven Parrot-Toy Categories are not hard and fast divisions. Just ask Baby, Carol's Umbrella cockatoo. He was given a large PVC-tube peanut hider. He promptly unfastened the quick link and dropped it to the floor of the cage where he proceeded to drag it along the bottom grate making as much noise as possible. It just shows—one parrot's food finder can be another's noisemaker. He had no intention of trying to remove the peanuts—he just loved the racket it made!

 **CHEEP! CHEEP!**

- Try stuffing food items into clean pinecones. Parrots have a great time trying to dislodge the food—and then chewing up the pinecone.

- Weave large leaves of greens such as kale, spinach, or turnip greens through the cage bars. If they are wet, it's an added bonus to those parrots that like to "leaf bathe." String dried wheel pasta; mini pretzels; cheerios, etc. on a skewer.

- *Rawhide-a-Nut*—Boil water and add some food coloring if desired. Place a knot or roll of rawhide into the boiling water until it softens. Cut holes big enough to squeeze in nuts appropriate for your bird. Nuts such as pistachios, almonds, filberts, or even sunflower seeds can be used. Let dry. Your parrot will enjoy working to dislodge the tasty morsels. This same idea can be applied to a block of wood. Nuts can be wedged into holes drilled into the block. Small blocks can be foot toys—large blocks can be hung in the cage.

- Small boxes of cereal (cornflakes is a good one) and the little snack size boxes of raisins make an inexpensive, ready-made Food Finder. Birds can hang onto a box, tear into it to get the goodies, and then shred the box up too.

- *Peek-a-Treat*—Cut a small hole in an appropriate size box for your bird. Let your buddy see you put nuts, peanuts, popcorn or any other yummy treat inside. He gets the fun of trying to get the treat out.

- Cut a coconut in half and hang half in your bird's cage using a parrot-safe method. Parrots, especially the larger ones, will enjoy eating the coconut out of the shell. Watch for spoliage.

- *Coconut Surprise*—Use a nail to poke a hole in the top of a coconut and drain the milk. Cut open the coconut (use a chop saw or poke holes around middle and break it open with a hammer). Scoop out the flesh and save it for later. Poke a hole in the top and bottom halves of the coconut. The holes need to be large enough so chain or leather will easily slide through. Run a piece of parrot-safe chain or leather through both cocount halves long enough so your parrot can slide the top half up and down on the chain of leather, to get his treats. If you are using chain, a small piece of leather or cotton rope looped through the bottom chain link will keep the bottom half of the coconut from sliding off. You now have a great treat hider. Let your bird watch you hide the goodies at first. You might also let part of the treat be visible so he gets the idea of where to look.

- *Crunchy Roll*—*Lightly* spread peanut butter on a paper towel roll then roll it in raisins, dried fruit, granola, crunchy cereal, or whatever tickles your parrot's fancy. Hang it in the cage and watch your parrot get busy! (Always watch for the ingestion of nonfood material.)

- *Spoon Treats*—Spread a thin layer of peanut butter in the bowl of a wooden kitchen spoon. Spoons can be bought in packs of three or more at grocery and dollar stores. Press in some granola, pellets, crunchy cereal, dried fruit, etc. It's great fun to eat the treat and then destroy the spoon!

- ***Roll-o'-Treat***—Hide a treat such as a nut in a cardboard paper towel roll. Bend both ends shut and push between the cage bars. This is a favorite of Carol's four macaws. Everyone waits in eager anticipation as a peanut is hidden with much fanfare in each tube. As each one is handed out, it's all business as the peanuts are discovered and eaten.

- ***Parrot Piñata***—Fill a paper bag with fun treats, blow into it to 'poof' it up, tie with a strip of leather and hang in the cage.

Preeners

To keep their feathers in tip-top shape, parrots preen themselves and also each other.

FOR EXAMPLE...

Preeners are parrot toys that can be preened, chewed, shredded, or woven. Often a bird will sit on his perch quietly chewing a leather strand that dangles nearby. These toys can also be great stress reducers. A Preener parrot toy may provide the added benefit of being a problem solver for those birds that over preen or pull their feathers. Examples of Preeners include parrot toys that are made of or contain peacock feathers, leather strands, cotton rope or jute, cloth strips, and woven palm strands. Parrots seem to enjoy different textures and parrot toys with a combination of these materials usually earn an avian "thumbs up." These are best hung close to a bird's face near a roosting or nighttime perch. Some of the Preener parrot toys consist of relatively long strands of jute, cloth, or leather. The Weavers especially will find these toys appealing.

CHEEP! CHEEP!

- A natural feather duster, natural whisk broom, or all-cotton mop head with the strings cut to about 3 inches, all can make good Preener parrot toys. A feather duster or mop head may be quite overwhelming to a smaller parrot if immediately placed inside its cage. Be sensitive to your bird and introduce these slowly. Always monitor birds with cotton rope.

Sunny, a Sun conure, is the official "store bird" of Wild Bird Center in Colorado Springs, Colorado. He would become visibly upset whenever Lauren, who was working there at the time, would dust the showroom with a pink feather duster. Finally she put it in his cage whereupon it immediately became Sunny's best buddy. Because Sunny didn't want anyone dusting the store with his *friend*, they just had to purchase another one!

- Strips of washed, brightly colored scrap cloth can be tied to cage bars, along leather strips, or knotted around metal, acrylic, or grape wreath rings. Interspersing the cloth with knotted pieces of leather, cotton rope, and jute will add some interesting textures. "Paper twist" found in craft stores used for making bows can be cut in lengths and tied onto cage bars or other parrot toys. Untwist the ends for a fun, 'poofy' Preener.

- Dried field corn (the kind you feed squirrels) can make a good Preener. There is a lot of beak activity required to pick off each kernel, manipulate it, and then drop it.

- Even something as simple as twists or strips of newspaper pushed between cage bars or woven through plastic chain can be a quick Preener parrot toy.

- *Tissue Flower*—Stack six pieces of facial tissue on top of each other. Put a bead, large button, or similar object in center. Draw up the tissue and tie snugly around the bead with a small piece of yarn or leather. Attach the flower to side cage bars near a perch. It's loads of fun to shred!

- *Raffia Knot*—Tie several strands of raffia or ribbon about 8 inches long in a knot around a cage bar. The strands can be used for preening.

- *Chain-o-Mania*—For this parrot toy you will need parrot-safe chain. An 8-inch length works well but you may vary it depending on the size of your bird, the amount of materials you have, and your patience. You will also need leather strips cut into 6- to 8-inch sections. Push a leather strip through each hole in the chain and knot both ends. Many birds love to undo the knots, pull the leather strips out, and chew them. You may also tie small wood blocks, spools, beads, etc. onto the leather to make a parrot toy filled with surprises. The chain may be hung from one end or strung across a corner of the cage with quick links.

Push-'n-Pulls

In the jungle, parrots pull, twist, and push branches, twigs, and leaves as they look for food.

FOR EXAMPLE...

Push-'n-Pulls are parrot toys in which pieces can slide back and forth or move up and down. These may also be mobiles that can be pushed and twirled, or "busy boards" of wood or acrylic that can be attached to the side of the cage. Abacus-type parrot toys may consist of one or more acrylic rods on which wood or plastic pieces move back and forth. Push 'n Pulls can provide a miniature physical workout in addition to mental stimulation as a parrot figures out what parts move. These parrot toys may be made of wood or acrylic so there might be some overlap with other categories.

CHEEP! CHEEP!

- ***Pull-Me Bead***—Cut a 1/2-inch board to a size suitable for your parrot. Drill several holes through the wood and one hole near the top for hanging. Thread a piece of leather or cotton rope through each hole. Tie a plastic bead or block of wood on each end of each piece to act as a stopping device. The ropes should be able to be pulled back and forth. Hang in the cage using a parrot-safe method.

- ***Busy-Beak Board***—Cut a piece of board in a size suitable to be attached to the side of your bird's cage. Pick the toys that you want to hang from the board. These should be smaller items such as a bell, pieces of leather or cloth, rawhide dog shoe, rawhide taco (see **Puzzler**), colored pieces of wood, pieces of cholla; plastic wiffle balls, etc.

  Design the toy spacing on the board by marking the spot where each toy will be placed. Attach screweyes to these spots. You may hang your toys using short pieces of leather, S-hooks (closed tightly), or quick links. Drill two holes through the board in line about 3 to 4 inches apart. Push two bolts through the board (bolts should be long enough to go through the board and clear the cage bars in the back). To attach the board to the cage, add a washer and wingnut to each bolt and tighten. The washer should be large enough to span the distance between two cage bars. Now watch the fun begin!

Movers and Shakers

The parrot's zygodactyl toe design (two toes forward and two toes backward) give it a remarkable ability to firmly grip branches and allow for all sorts of wondrous acrobatic feats.

Wheee!

FOR EXAMPLE...

Movers and Shakers include swings, ladders, rings, perch toys (toys with a hole to slide onto a perch), spiral perches, plastic chain, and knotted ropes. These parrot toys will really get your feathered friend swinging! There is no end to the variety in this category. These may be made from virtually any bird-safe material. Every parrot should have a **Movers and Shakers** in its cage at all times. The exercise potential is unlimited.

CHEEP! CHEEP!

- *Simple Perch Parrot Toy*—A perch parrot toy slides onto a perch and can be manipulated with foot or beak. For this one you will need an unfinished wooden curtain ring and three 6- to 8-inch long pieces of leather or jute. Keep all three pieces together and tie the ring into the center with one large knot. Knot beads, buttons, or small wooden pieces to the ends of each strand. Keep lengths of strands and beads appropriate for your size parrot. Slide the ring onto the perch.

- *Braided Ladder for Small Birds*—This is an easy ladder to make for the little guys such as budgies, cockatiels, and lovebirds. Knot together three strands of six-ply jute, sisal, or cotton cloth and braid tightly. Tie a knot at the end and attach a quick link to the top. Depending on the length, push dowels or small branches through the material every few inches. Keep these "rungs" relatively short. You may add beads as you braid the rope. Monitor this toy and if the braid becomes lose, remove from cage and redo.

- "Ball and Dowel" decorative hardwood trim for porches can be a cute ready-made ladder for medium size parrots. The spindle trim works well too. These are available at hardware stores.

- *Braided Swing for Small Birds*—Braid as described in the section on the braided ladder. Push a quick link through the *center* of the long braid. Push one long dowel or branch through both ends of the braid. Hang in your parrot's cage and away he goes!

- *The "Every-Bird-Should-Have-a-Swing" Swing*—
  For the actual swing use a dowel, branch, or piece of
  PVC of the appropriate diameter for your parrot. (If
  you are unsure about the correct diameter, turn to the
  section on the **Practically-Perfect-Parrot-
  Adventure Station** in the next chapter.) To hang the
  swing, use any bird-safe rope or chain. To attach the
  perch to the hanger, drill a hole down through the each
  end of the perch if it is of a large enough diameter or
  use screweyes in the ends. Screweyes can be pried open
  and the last link of a chain put through or ropes can be
  run through the screweye holes and knotted. Use your
  imagination and add small toys such as beads, wooden
  blocks, tied pieces of cloth or leather, and rawhide to
  the chain or rope that you use to hang your swing.
  Swings may be made to fit into a cage or to attach to a
  ceiling in a birdroom or out on a covered porch. "Baffles"
  will keep your parrot on his swing and not hanging
  from your rafters. See the hints in the next chapter on
  how to make a baffle.

- *Pyramid Swing*—For this swing you will need three
  dowels or branches. Attach screweyes to the cut ends of
  all three branches. Get three pieces of equal length bird-
  safe chain. Pry open one screweye on each branch.
  Attach the end of one piece of chain to each branch.
  Lay out branches in a triangle with the chain end of
  one branch next to unchained end of other. Attach the
  triangle together by closing the screweyes. Pull the
  three chains up to form the top of the pyramid. Attach
  all with a quick link. Depending on the width of the
  chain links, you may need to fasten them together with
  an "S" hook first, and then attach a quick link. Toys
  can be strung on the chain beforehand as in the above
  example. Check out the next chapter to see how to turn
  this pyramid swing into an inexpensive hanging play
  area!

- *Wreath Swing*—It's easy to make a great swing with a grape or willow wreath purchased at a craft store. Be sure the wreath is not stained or painted before purchasing. You may add additional interest by tying on pieces of cloth and leather, a bell, and wooden blocks to chew. Wreaths may be hung from the top or hung flat by tying it in three places and drawing the leather, cord, or chain up to form a pyramid.

- *Coat Hanger or Ring Swing*—Bend a coat hanger into a circle or use a plastic, metal, or wooden ring suitable for your parrot. Beginning at one end, wrap six-ply jute or cotton rope *tightly* around the ring covering it completely. If using a hanger, wrap everything except for the hanger part. Tie the ends securely and hang in the cage. Always monitor, and if the wrapping becomes loose, remove and rewrap.

Foot Toys

Again, that unique toe design with two toes forward and two back provides a parrot with a "fist" with which to hold things. The beak also is used as an extra "hand."

FOR EXAMPLE...

Foot Toys are small parrot toys that are suitable for grasping. These may be items such as small pieces of wood, rattles, barbells, hard rubber chews, rawhide pieces, small chunks of cholla, and hard plastic toys that roll and wobble. Foot toys can go into the toy bowl or toy chest in the cage. They're great to have on hand as a beak distraction to keep your parrot from nibbling on your fingers. And they are fun to play with on the floor. Some parrots love to play on their backs and wrestle with their Foot Toys.

Lauren's friend's conure "Sitaboria" never goes to the bottom of his cage to play except when he's given a plastic Easter egg filled with beads. Then he and his egg can be heard rolling and playing for hours.

CHEEP! CHEEP!

- *Let's Go Shopping*—This a cute game to play with your parrot and his Foot Toys. Put some Foot Toys in a little box or basket on the bed or floor. You and your buddy can "go shopping" in the basket for his favorite things.

- *Crunchies*—Save the chewed up bits of wood from hanging toys and recycle these "crunchies" to be used as Foot Toys in your bird's toy bowl. One bird's trash is another's treasure, especially if you have different size birds.

- Some human baby toys make good Foot Toys such as hard plastic rattles and plastic keys on a ring.

- Compressed grain or vegetable dog bones and rawhide bones and shoes make fun Foot Toys for larger parrots. Plastic bottle caps (remove the blue liner first), ball-point pen caps, wireless clothespins, and popsicle sticks will keep the medium and smaller parrots happy.

- *Silly Sacks*—Cut clean brightly colored cloth into 6- to 8-inch squares. Place a small item or two such as beads, sticks, or crinkled paper in the center. Fold it in half, fold in the sides, and tie snugly with a small strip of cloth.

The Toy Chest

Let's see...what shall I play with now...hmmmm???

FOR EXAMPLE...

This last category isn't really a parrot toy but rather a box, bowl, or container that may be placed inside the cage allowing your bird to pick out his own foot toys to play with. The Toy Chest is a good place to put the chunks of old toys that still have some "chew" left in them. It is simple to designate a bowl in the cage as a "toy bowl."

Baby, the Umbrella Cockatoo, has one and this is the first place he looks when he returns to his cage. There is always something *new* to chew in there. Toy bowls, boxes, and baskets provide another place to "forage" which keeps bird brains busy! A larger toy chest placed *underneath* the cage can be a handy storage place for your bird's recycled parrot toys. Most toy chests may be made from something around the house, but there are some nice wooden and plastic containers on the market too for under the cage. A wooden bucket (no staples or nails) purchased at a hobby shop can make a cute toy chest.

Last but not least—
STUPID TOYS

Just because these are being sold as parrot toys doesn't mean that they are fun, safe, or stimulating.

- Toys on thin chain with cheap bells and large pieces of manzanita wood. Small parrots can't chew the wood, and the bell and chain are dangerous for large parrots. Who is this toy made for?

- Any parrot toy in which all the wood is manzanita. This wood is too hard for most parrots.

- Any parrot toy designated for large parrots with cheap bells with dangerous clappers.

- The use of pear links on toys made for macaws and large cockatoos.

- Acrylic ladders made with string to hold the rungs.

- Anything that uses jingle bells—because of the openings in the bells, it is easy for a bird to get their beak or toenail caught.

12 SHOPPING SPREE

Need some parrot toys in a hurry? You don't even have to make a special trip to the bird store. Next time you're out shopping, look for these items that make great, inexpensive parrot toys. (Remember—not all of the items mentioned below are appropriate for all sizes or ages of parrots.)

Grocery Store:

*   Food as toys: whole ear of corn with husk, day-old bagel (great to hang or hold) sugar cane, whole carrots.

*   Infant toys such as plastic keys on a ring, hard plastic teething ring, a ringing phone , wooden baby blocks painted with non-toxic paint, plastic "links."

*   Dog rawhide in different shapes.

*   Natural whisk broom (see **Preener**).

*   Natural all-cotton mop heads (see **Preener**)

*   Natural feather duster (see **Preener**).

*   Coconut to cut for a treat-hider (see **Food Finder**).

*   Wooden spoons.

*   Cotton gloves for a "Glove Surprise" (see **Food Finder**).

*   Package of corks.

*   Dixie cups.

*   Roll of paper towel or toilet paper.

*   Box of white tissues.

Craft Shop:

- Wireless clothespins—regular size and mini.

- Wooden spoons, popsicle sticks, skill sticks, craft sticks.

- Wooden shapes such as spools, miniature flowerpots, wheels, balls, rings, wooden "Christmas lights", hearts, etc. Many of these have holes drilled in them ready for stringing or to use as a foot toy. Avoid any cut shapes made of pressed wood or plywood.

- Bags of wood scraps.

- Plastic beads—animals, hearts, stars, etc. Avoid colored wooden beads as the paint is toxic. Most plastic beads sold will be appropriate for toys for smaller birds only.

- Pre-packaged strips of cloth for use in Preener parrot toys.

- Cloth "craft loops" which can be cut and added to toys.

- All-wood baskets, trucks, boats, etc. Be sure there are no staples or nails. These can be toys themselves or used to hold toys.

- Natural willow or grapevine wreaths to use as swings. A small willow heart makes a cute cockatiel or lovebird swing when hung upside down. Be sure the willow or grapevine is natural, not moldy, and not coated or painted. Don't use straw as this is held together with nylon.

- Natural raffia—short lengths are great for weaving through cage bars.

- Natural feathers such as peacock.

- Blond willow baskets of all sorts. Cockatiels love to chew the little ones.

- Large willow baskets, unpainted wooden children's toy chests, or wicker picnic baskets can be used for a parrot-toy chest underneath the cage.

- Paper twist, as well as raffia, knotted leather strands, cloth, or jute can be used to jazz up old parrot toys.

Hardware Store:
- Large nuts and bolts made of nylon or stainless steel.

- Plastic chain.

- Untreated scrap wood that can be cut into small pieces.

- Unfinished pine finials, wood curtain rod rings, and balls. These can be drilled to use in Destructible parrot toys for the larger birds.

As you can see, the **Eleven Parrot-Toy Categories** can serve as a guide to providing your feathered friend with the widest array of entertaining and stimulating parrot toys. Whether you buy or build, the choice is yours. But the end result will be the same—a healthy and happy companion parrot! Have Fun!

PART 2

Play Areas:
The Ticket To Adventure

THE PARROT
PHYSIQUE GYM

A LITTLE STORY...

Ali Macaw, the Blue and Gold macaw, caught everyone's eye as she strutted into the Parrot Physique Gym.

"I'm here to use my free pass to see if I'll like the Wings of Steel program," she smiled as she extended her shapely wing to PJ the young male Eclectus at the front counter. Ali was getting tired of hanging around her cage all day. She wanted someplace she could go to meet some cool guys and stay in shape too.

"Yes, ma'am," he stammered. "Right this way." "Wow, what a babe!" he thought.

As Ali sauntered by the mirror on the way to the gym, she rezipped a tail feather that had become mussed and tossed her brilliant blue plumage. Finally, she arrived at the play area. It was time to get to work. She noticed immediately that the gym had many different levels. Climbing up and down was giving her a great aerobic workout. There was plenty of room for stretching and reaching as she lunged for one of the tempting parrot toys hanging just out of reach.

"And a swing, too. This place is all right!" she thought.

After working out for awhile, Ali was getting thirsty so she headed over to the Juice and Snack Bar for a healthy drink. As she took a sip from her bowl, she glanced at the gym next to her. There before her eyes was the most gorgeous hunk of a Blue and Gold she'd ever seen. His yellow chest was broad, his blue feathers glistening as he pumped his parrot dumbbell. His name was Bubba. Her decision was made—she was going to join the Parrot Physique Gym!

1 AN OUT-OF-CAGE EXPERIENCE

How would you like to transform your cranky conure into a contented cuddlebug? Or turn your beefy Blue-Front into a svelte psittacine? Got a bored Blue and Gold that could use a little parrot pizzazz?

All parrots benefit from time spent **away** from their cages. Because of their intelligence, our pet birds enjoy new learning experiences. Getting out of the cage and into a different environment can be stimulating and exciting. Sharing your life with your feathered buddy is more enjoyable when he's got his own place away from his cage to hang out and watch the fun. Besides, sitting behind bars all day can really get to be a drag!

Expand your parrot's world—give him an out-of-cage experience!

2 HEADMATES

So you've gotten your feathered dynamo out of his cage. Now what? Your bird can sit *on you* during his jaunts around the house. This, however, isn't always the safest or most convenient option. Here are three reasons why:

1. Like a young child, a parrot has a very short attention span. A bored parrot hanging out on your arm or shoulder will soon find shirt buttons or earrings mighty enticing. And just as with a small   child, a constant stream of "No! No!" eventually loses its effectiveness and wears on your patience.

2.   Parrots are by nature inquisitive but destructive creatures. Even setting a bird down "for a minute" on the back of a chair, table top, or floor can result in chewed woodwork or worse. It is only fair to your feathered companion to give him a parrot-safe location that protects him *and* your valuables.

3.   Some pet birds spend a lot of time riding around on their human's shoulder. They have come to believe that this is their rightful spot. Besides encouraging boredom (see #1 above) it can also be dangerous. In the parrot world, **he who is highest is boss.**

When a parrot sits on your shoulder you have allowed him to be at the same height or, in the case of the larger parrots, higher than your head. Your face and head are the most important parts of your body to your bird. Sitting on your shoulder he will *bond* to your head and see it as a fellow creature.

In the wild, a parrot sitting next to its "mate" would snuggle next to it, preen it, and **warn it when danger approaches** with a bite that says, "Fly off to safety!" If someone approaches you that your bird views as *danger* (this could be a spouse, child, or other pet), like a good mate your parrot will try to protect you with a warning bite. This is often interpreted as aggression when in reality it is meant as protection. Unfortunately, not having feathers to cushion the bite, people often suffer unpleasant results. Don't be a **headmate**.

3 INTRODUCING... THE PARROT ADVENTURE STATION!

The safest and most convenient way to provide an out-of-cage experience is by providing your feathered companion with a **Parrot Adventure Station (PAS)**. A PAS is a parrot-safe structure—either moveable or stationary—that is located **away from the cage** and provides opportunities for exercise, playing with parrot toys, interaction with family members, and other out-of-cage experiences. Sound like fun? You bet it is!

It is important to mention here that a PAS is not a substitute for a cage. Every parrot needs a cage for safety and security. If you have just acquired a bird, your first priority should be to provide your pet with a safe, easily maintained cage of the correct size. Then read on to learn about parrot adventure stations and what they can provide for you and your feathered companion.

PARROT ADVENTURE STATION VARIETIES:

- **Perches**—Perches and T-stands are the simplest PAS and are available for any size parrot. These tend to be the most portable of the PAS. Even the back of a discarded chair can serve as a PAS. Decide on your primary use when purchasing a perch or T-stand. If you want your parrot to join you for dinner, you might chose a perch with a large tray to catch food. Sitting next to you as you work on the computer may require just a simple T-stand. For the larger parrot, a freestanding model that prevents access to the floor may make more sense than a tabletop version. Also included in this category are shower perches that adhere to the shower walls with suction cups.

- **Gyms**—These may be made of wood, PVC, or a combination. They may be large freestanding models or small tabletop models. Gyms usually have several "levels" and may even include ladders and swings. Take into account the following when considering a gym: How easy it is to keep clean? Does it have a "skirt"? If you are going to take it from room to room, will it fit through the doorways? What are the space requirements? How tall is it? How durable is it? Can you get replacement parts if needed? Where are parrot toys hung? Can it be customized for your particular parrot?

- **Tree stands**—These are usually large manzanita trees on bases. Tree stands make very impressive parrot adventure stations—like having a tree growing in our living room just for your feathered friend! The branches provide a great natural climbing experience. Tree stands tend to be heavy and somewhat awkward to move around. When purchasing, consider the sanded vs. the unsanded varieties. The unsanded manzanita can be slick and the dark color a little more disconcerting to some birds.

- **Hanging play areas**—These include any play structures that can be hung from the ceiling. They can be a hanging basket, branches, a swing, a spiral perch, or trays with perches, swings and ladders. Hanging play areas provide the perfect PAS for people with minimal floor space. They are also ideal for homes with toddlers or dogs.

BENEFITS OF A PARROT ADVENTURE STATION:

- **T**ime for fun—Getting away from its cage and out where the action is can be fun and exciting for your feathered friend. It can be a time to share the family dinner, take a shower, or just hang out. Gyms and T-stands should be outfitted with plenty of parrot toys. (It's a great way to recycle parrot toys from the cage.) The time spent out on the PAS could even include something special such as a favorite treat or well-liked parrot toy.

- **I**nteraction— Parrots are social creatures. They thrive on interaction with others and want to be included as part of the group. In the wild, many parrots spend the day in a **flock** traveling, eating, playing, and resting. **You** are your parrot's **flock** and your bird looks forward to spending time with you. With a PAS you can include your feathered companion in family activities. A gym in the family room, a T-stand alongside the dinner table, or a perch near the computer allows social time with the family. A parrot that feels included tends to be quieter and calmer. Isolation can promote screaming.

- **C**ontrol—Notice that we did not include **cage top** play areas in the list of parrot adventure stations. It's ok for an occasional romp, but birds that play exclusively *on top* of their cages can become **territorial**, resorting to biting and chasing if anyone invades their space. Parrots that spend an inordinate amount of time *in* their cage can become **cage-bound** and very fearful of leaving that environment. Spending time on a PAS that is located **away** from the cage expands your companion's "world" and ultimately helps you maintain better control over his behavior.

- **K**ey to Safety—A PAS provides a **parrot-safe** location where your pet can spend quality time with his "flock." A bird with access to the floor or furniture can wreak havoc in a very short time. A parrot on the loose is a danger to family members and to himself. **Set yourself up for success** and provide your feathered companion with a safe, controlled place to play and interact with the rest of the family.

- **E**xercise—Like the "Parrot Physique Gym" in the opening story, a PAS can be a great place to **exercise** (and meet other cool parrots!). Exercise is critical for all parrots, especially for high-energy macaws and cockatoos. A few hours climbing around a gym can do wonders for a noisy, restless parrot. It can also burn off some extra calories for that "perch potato" in the flock.

- **T**hrive—A PAS provides another **foraging area**. Parrots in the wild spend the day going from place to place looking or foraging for food. Traveling to different areas is mentally and physically stimulating for a parrot. A PAS can provide an **alternate** environment in your home for "foraging", playing with parrot toys, and new adventures. Diversity is healthy and a healthy parrot is a happy parrot.

A parrot adventure station is your parrot's **T-I-C-K-E-T** to Fun!

4 WINGS OF STEEL

Unlike their wild cousins who spend their days busy with the business of survival, our companion parrots lead a pretty sedentary life. In nature, the search for food alone often involves flying for miles, scrapping with companions for the choicest morsels, dexterity and acrobatics. In captivity, all this is accomplished with the plop of a bowl in the cage. It's awfully easy for our feathered friends to become "perch potatoes!" That is why exercise is so important for your bird. A little "birdie aerobics" every day can burn off excess energy, reduce stress, and help keep your psittacine svelte.

Turn your PAS into your bird's very own Parrot Physique Gym by engaging him in activities that increase his heart rate and get him "movin' and shakin."Here are some ideas:

- Play "**Come and Get Me**." Go from one end of the PAS to the other and encourage him to come and get you.

- If you can outfit your PAS with a long ladder, let him spend some time climbing. If he ends up on the floor, have him climb the ladder to get back on his PAS.

- Anything that encourages swinging and flapping is great. Do some flapping exercises with him before he goes on his PAS. Hold him firmly over your head and drop your arm to get him to flap.

- Play **Toss**. Use a wadded up piece of paper, wooden ball, or anything he can get his beak on. He throws it—you retrieve it. (Actually this will probably be a work out for you too!) Some birds can learn to catch a soft, lightweight ball. Lauren's foster Umbrella Cockatoo Bubba loves to play tug-of-war with a long twisted piece of newspaper. Eventually he wins and gets to rip it up. "Toss the paper wad" is also one of Bubba's favorites.

- Get creative and you and your buddy will be able to think up all sorts of outrageous and fun things to stay in shape. Carol and her Umbrella Baby have invented a crazy game called "Elephant Nose" that involves a paper towel roll. Baby holds one end in her beak and Carol holds the other end up to her mouth and toots through it. Together the two of them whip back and forth in tandem with Baby getting crazier by the minute. When they're both pooped, Baby gets to chew up the roll!

5 SAFETY FIRST!

Now that you are all set to give your companion parrot a "home away from home", give some thought to PAS location and safety. Here are some tips:

1. Place the PAS out of the main traffic flow of the room. For a bird that is easily frightened, backing the PAS up to a wall can make him feel more secure. Kids and dogs running around a PAS can be stressful to a bird and can cause him to spend as much time flying off the stand as on it.

2. Be sure the immediate area is parrot-safe. Watch for ceiling fans, open windows, and outside doors. Avoid hot surfaces such as stoves and fireplaces. Keep dangerous items out of reach. These include poisonous plants, chemicals, stained glass, valuables, and furniture. Provide plenty of parrot toys to keep inquisitive beaks occupied.

3. Unless you are prepared to make the considerable commitment to owning a flighted parrot, your bird's **wing feathers** should always be **trimmed**, especially if he will be spending time out of his cage. A flying parrot can crash into mirrors, windows, and sliding glass doors. Worse yet, an escape through an open outside door could mean that you have lost your feathered friend forever.

4. If you take your bird into the **bathroom** on a T-stand, be aware of open toilets, cosmetics, and fumes from perfume, hairspray, and nail polish remover. Because

a parrot's respiratory system is seven times more sensitive than ours is, avoid spraying anything in the vicinity of your parrot. Also remember that in the shower, perches can be slippery when wet.

5.   Always **supervise** your bird when he is out on his PAS. Don't take chances. Be especially vigilant when other pets are in the vicinity.

Just about every parrot will at some time or another end up cruising the carpet rather than sitting on his PAS. If you run into this problem, ask yourself these questions:

•   Is he being frightened? See #1 above.

•   Is he hungry or thirsty? If your parrot spends at least one hour out on his PAS, he should have access to food and water.

•   Is he bored? He should have access to plenty of parrot toys. Parrots have short attention spans. Anticipate this and intervene with something new or exciting before he gets antsy.

•   Are you around? Your parrot wants to know where you are and be with you. Hanging out with his flock is a top priority. If you leave and he screams, answer his "contact call" with a reassuring word that you will be right back. If you disappear, he may get off his PAS and come looking for you.

•   Is he tired? Has he been out too long and is it time to go back to his cage?

Sometimes parrots end up on the floor because they are playing hard and may lose their footing. Carol's Lilac-Crowned Amazon Tucker loves to do battle with the parrot toys hanging on his gym. It is not unusual for him swipe so hard at something that he tumbles right off the PAS. He will look around in confusion as if to say, "How did I end up down here?"

6 THE GOLDEN RULE

Always REMEMBER
The Rule of 3

When confronted with a wandering Polly, always remember the **"Rule of Three."** If you have asked yourself all the questions listed above and offered solutions, then the *third* time down means that it is time to do something different and leave the PAS. Give your bird a shower, engage in some flapping exercise, or take him back to the cage for some rest and relaxation (R&R). Don't get angry or make a big deal of it. It just means that your buddy is ready for something else.

You may have to actually *train* your parrot to stay on his PAS. If this is the case, you might want to ignore the "Rule of Three" for awhile and put your bird back up on his play area more often in an effort to teach him that this is where the fun is and wandering the carpet is a "no-no." Once you feel that he's gotten the message, then you can use the Rule of Three as a guideline.

Make the time spent on a PAS fun, interesting, and nonthreatening. Parrots learn through the **positive reinforcement** of **correct** behavior rather than from punishment. This means that you will see more positive results by getting into the habit of saying "Good bird!" whenever you catch your pal on his PAS playing, exercising, or just hanging out and looking cool. A constant barrage of "Bad bird!" if he ends up on the floor—or for that matter any time he does something inappropriate—accomplishes nothing except raising your blood pressure. The greater the issue you make over something, the greater the chance your bird will learn to repeat those behaviors. These are smart creatures and they love drama! The key to successful parrot behavior is to make a fuss over **positive behaviors**, not negative ones. Try it and your buddy will love you!

7 IT'S COMPLETELY BAFFLING

Some of you may live with an *avian acrobat* who can easily slide down a pole to the floor or climb up a chain to nibble on the ceiling. In this case it may be necessary to *baffle* the escape route. A **baffle** is a physical barrier that is too large to climb around or grip. An appropriate baffle will depend on the size and agility of your parrot. Some things that may work as baffles are: plastic lids, margarine tubs, pie pans, Frisbees, and a funnel. Punch or drill a hole in the center of your baffle and thread your PAS hanging chain or playgym leg through. A 1 to 2 foot section of 2 to 3-inch diameter PVC pipe is also an effective baffle. Fastened to a chain or leg, it is too wide for most parrots to grip. Some of the baffles that are sold to keep squirrels out of outdoor bird feeders will also work very nicely on a PAS.

8 BEAKER, I'D LIKE TO INTRODUCE YOU TO....

Some parrots will be all over their new PAS immediately, while others may need a more prolonged introduction. It may take some pet birds several days or even longer to be bold enough to extend that first cautious toe. Be patient and proceed slowly. Here are some tips if your bird is a little suspicious of his new apparatus.

• Drape yourself over it and "ooh" and "aah."

• Hang his absolutely favorite parrot toy from it.

- Hang his absolutely favorite food item from it.

- Leave it in the vicinity for several days; walk by it often with your bird.

- Use a "model" bird that is not afraid to explore.

- Lay it on its side on the floor and begin playing with it at this angle.

- Let your parrot make initial contact and explore with his *beak* only for awhile.

Always have a "happy face" and calm demeanor. Make a "big fuss" over *any* positive progress..."Good Bird!"

9 WHO'S THE BOSS HERE?

And now a word on height. Is there any such thing as a PAS that is too high? Well, that depends! Remember earlier in the chapter we made the statement that **he who is highest is boss**? In the world of parrots, this is a very important rule. In a flock of birds the easiest way to tell who is dominant is to see who is sitting on the highest branch. Parrots in the wild will often vie for top position. They will do this in the living room too. Have you ever taken your pet bird out of his cage only to have him immediately run up your arm to your shoulder? He's heading for the highest spot.

Height is Might

The general rule is that a your feathered friend should **sit no higher than your head**. Birds that consistently perch above their humans tend to be nippy and harder to control. They just don't want to give up that alpha position! There are those of you who are probably saying, "But my Beaker always sits higher than me and I never have any problem with him!" And you might be right. If you own a placid Polly then rejoice. But for those with the cantankerous cockatoo or mischievous macaw, take heed. Just about every parrot wants to be Top Dog!

When designing or buying a parrot adventure station, keep this critical issue of height in mind. Legs can be shortened or perches lowered. Base your decisions on the personality of your parrot, how long he will be out on his PAS, and the height of each person who will interact with him. Safety is also an important consideration. If you must keep your feathered friend out of the reach of dogs or toddlers, then compromise on the height. One technique is to **raise the person up** to the level of the parrot with a stool when they wish to interact.

This reminds us of a situation—we like to call the "macaw-spouse syndrome"—that is pretty common. One spouse (usually the husband) acquires a large parrot (usually a macaw) and immediately places him at a height that is appropriate for him but is too high for the spouse (usually the wife) to comfortably reach. After a little while of looking *down* on the wife and kids, the parrot begins to think of himself as King of the Hill. He starts to misbehave and bite when they try to handle him. After all, he's been given the alpha position. So a word to the wise. Be sure the *humans* in the flock come out on top!

10 ADVENTURE TIME

So you and your buddy are ready for adventure! Here are some great things to do on a Parrot Adventure Station:

- sing crazy songs
- dance to music
- have a newspaper rip-a-thon
- take a shower
- watch a video/TV
- have dinner with the flock
- share a snack
- go visit a friend's house
- go to work
- share quiet time together
- work on the computer
- help fold clothes
- play catch with a wiffle ball
- wash dishes
- what can you think of to do?

11 CHEEP! CHEEP!

Open up any pet bird magazine or catalog
and you will find an enticing array of gyms,
towers, treestands, and perches. They come in a
variety of styles, sizes, and prices. For those of
you low on cash or long on creativity, we have
provided ideas for Parrot Adventure Stations that
you can make yourself. Included are items you may have
around the house or yard, things you can buy and set up, and
fancier PVC gyms you can build. With all the great ideas,
there's no reason that your feathered friend can't have several
PAS located throughout the house! So get creative and have
some fun!

- **Instant Little Bird** PAS—A wooden clothes drying
  rack makes a quick and easy play stand for lovebirds,
  cockatiels, parakeets, or small conures. A wooden dish
  drying rack would make a tabletop version. These are
  easy to put in tubs or sinks for birdie showers.

- **Bird in a Basket**—Purchase a handled wicker basket
  of the appropriate size for your parrot. Wrap the
  handle tightly and completely in jute. This portable
  basket PAS can sit on a table or be suspended from the
  ceiling. (Use a parrot safe hanging method from the
  previous chapter on parrot toys). Your bird can sit on
  the handle and play with his foot parrot toys that are
  stored in the basket. Parrot toys can also be hung from
  the handle and the outside rim of the basket.

- **Suspended Parrot Adventure Stations**: If you have
  minimal floor space to devote to a Parrot Adventure
  Station then a suspended PAS may be the answer.
  Use a parrot-safe hanging method as described in the
  chapter on parrot toys. Here are three fun ideas:

1.   **The Giant Grape Wreath Swing**. Even the little guys will enjoy a giant grape wreath on which to swing and chew. Tie strips of leather, bright cloth, and small wooden parrot toys on the wreath for added interest.

2.   **Natural Tree Branches**. Choose some with multiple branches and you can make an exciting "hanging tree." Climbing around the branches and chewing the wood and bark will keep your feathered dynamo busy for hours. Add additional parrot toys, cotton "tightropes," and ladders for even more fun. See the chapter on parrot toys for a list of parrot-safe wood and how to collect it.

3.   **Hookbill Hodgepodge**. Swings you purchase or make yourself, spiral perches, rings, ladders, or any combination of these things suspended from the ceiling can make an exciting play area.

Don't forget a **Splat Mat** under your PAS. Splat Mats will keep carpets and surrounding areas clean. Splat Mats can be newspapers, old sheets that can be rewashed, plastic or fabric drop cloths, vinyl carpet runners, and carpet remnants. No self-respecting parrot can get through the day without being just a little bit messy! After all, flinging food in the jungle helps to replant next season's dinner. So use a Splat Mat under your PAS and cleaning up will be a breeze.

12 CHEEP! CHEEP! (CONT'D)

The following Parrot Adventure Station are made of **PVC** pipe. The white "drinking-water-quality" type PVC (white-SCH 40) is the one recommended for making parrot playgyms. PVC can typically be found in the plumbing or irrigation section of most hardware stores. PVC is great because it is inexpensive, easy to work with, and virtually indestructible as far as your parrot is concerned. One thing to keep in mind when shopping for PVC pipe and PVC connectors is to *be flexible* in your design. If you can't find a particular diameter pipe or connector, get creative and compromise somewhat on your plan. **Reducing connectors and slip bushings** will allow you to change diameters of the PVC pipe on your gym. A variety of perch diameters and materials are beneficial for your feathered friend so don't be afraid to mix and match if necessary.

To get you started, the following tools are recommended:

☑   **PVC pipe cutter or hacksaw**—A hacksaw is probably the most inexpensive way to go and does the job quite nicely. If you purchase a pipe cutter be sure that it will cut the larger diameter PVC if you are making a gym for a large parrot. Because the cutting produces an odor, do this well away from your bird.

☑   **Drill**—You will need this for drilling holes for screweyes to hang parrot toys, anchoring wooden dowels if you use them, and for mounting casters.

☑   **Measuring tape and marking pen.**

☑   **Rubber mallet**—Use this to tap the PVC into the connectors if necessary.

☑   **Sandpaper, palm sander, or belt sander**—Use any of these to *rough up* the PVC perches for a better grip for your bird. Plain PVC pipe is slippery. If you use a belt sander, you can *scallop* the perches for even better results.

☑   **Optional**—PVC cement. If you choose to cement your gym together, be aware that the fumes arc harmful to you and your parrot. All gluing should be done outside or in a well-ventilated area away from your parrot. Do not allow your bird on the gym until the cement has thoroughly dried. These gyms will stay together without gluing, and you may want to consider not using it if you intend to take the gym apart to transport it. One option is to cement just the base pieces together. Lightly sanding the pipe's surface will remove the red lettering if this is a concern.

The Basic T-stand

This is a simple lightweight T-stand. Pull the whole thing apart and you can transport it anywhere.

You will need:

❏ 8 feet of 1¼-inch PVC pipe for the base and upright. Cut four 10-inch pieces, two 8" pieces, and one 3-foot section. The 3-foot section is the upright and you can vary this length depending on how high you want your bird to sit. As a rule of thumb, keep your parrot at about your chest level.

❏ Three 1¼-inch 3-way connectors

❏ Four 1¼-inch caps

❏ Perch—Give some thought to the type of perch that will best suit the needs of you and your parrot. If you intend to use the T-stand in the shower, then a PVC perch well roughed up with a sander will be the most appropriate. Use a comfortable diameter PVC pipe for your pet. Refer to the section (*see* page 85) on **"The Practically-Perfect Parrot-Adventure-Station Playgym,"** for suggested diameters.

For the Perch you will need:

❏ Two 1-foot sections plus two caps of the correct diameter to fit the ends. If you will not be using 1¼-inch diameter PVC for your perch (we recommend this only for the largest parrots) you will need a 3-way **reducing connector or slip bushing** at the junction of the upright and perch that will accommodate the diameter perch you have chosen. A wooden dowel could be substituted for the PVC. If the dowel does not fit tightly, anchor it with a screw drilled up through the connector.

❑   Another option is to make a perch with a 1x2 piece of wood or a natural branch. In this case, eliminate the top 3-way connector and replace with a PVC cap. Screw your wooden perch or branch directly into the top of the cap. You can buy either metal or plastic parrot cups that come with a bolt that screws into the bottom. Drill a hole through the end of your perch and bolt the cup on.

❑   Assemble as shown in the diagram below, tapping with a rubber mallet if necessary to get a secure fit.

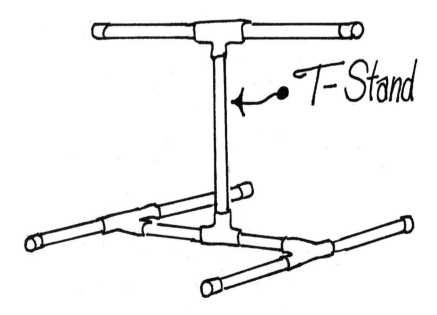

T-Stand

Litter Pan Perch with Parrot-Toy Holder

This simple tabletop PVC perch is built to fit in a kitty litter pan. Droppings and debris end up in the pan and not all over the table. Line the pan with newspaper or paper towels and cleanup is a snap!

Decide on the diameter PVC that is appropriate for your parrot. Refer to the section (*see* page 85) on **"The Practically Perfect Parrot Adventure Station Playgym,"** for suggested sizes. One option is to construct the stand of PVC and use a wooden dowel for the perch itself. If you decide to use PVC as a perch, be sure to sand it or wrap it in jute to ensure good footing.

You will need:

☐ Six 90° elbow connectors, three 3-way connectors, one screweye (with the "eye" large enough to accept the size of quick link you use on your parrot toys); and approximately 6½ feet of PVC pipe. The size of the litter pan and the diameter of the PVC will determine the exact measurements of the perch. We will give you the basic guidelines and then you will have to use your creative genius to complete the task! Don't worry—the fit doesn't have to be perfect.

☐ Lay four of the 90° elbow connectors in the corners of the pan and two of the 3-way connectors on the bottom in the approximate position that they will be in the finished product. Using a tape measurer, measure the lengths of PVC that you will have to cut for the bottom. The PVC pipe will extend up into *each* of the connectors about ½-inch or so. Be sure to take this into consideration when doing your measurements. Cut the pipe for the bottom and assemble. It was a perfect fit, right?

☐ The uprights that hold the perch should extend several inches above the lip of the pan; 6 to 8 inches above is recommended but do what will work for your parrot. A younger bird may be more comfortable on a lower perch. Cut the uprights and add them to the base. Top one with a 90° elbow connector and the other with a 3-way connector. Measure across for the perch, again being sure to take into consideration the extra ½-inch of pipe that will extend into *each* of the connectors. If you use a wooden dowel, anchoring it with a screw drilled up from the bottom of the connector will keep it from turning if it isn't a tight fit.

☐ The upright on the parrot toy holder should be several inches higher than your bird. Eight inches for the cross piece generally works well. Cut those pieces. Add the screweye to the cross piece. Push them into the 3-way connector then get your feathered buddy so you both can admire your handiwork!

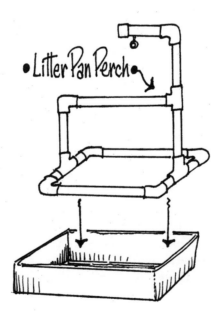

• Litter Pan Perch •

13 NOW PRESENTING...THE PRACTICALLY-PERFECT PARROT-ADVENTURE-STATION PLAYGYM

Here is a gym-style PAS that you can build in about 2 hours for approximately $20 to $50 depending on the size. Take a look at these eight outstanding features:

- Many gyms are too tall. A parrot ends up sitting at the highest point, which is usually above the owner's head. The Practically-Perfect-PAS is about 5 feet tall and arranged to keep your parrot at a manageable level.

- The Practically-Perfect-PAS is big on "playability." The design encourages movement and exploration.

- The perches and play area are positioned to keep droppings and mess confined to the center area and off surrounding floor.

- The design allows for parrot toys to be placed where your bird can reach and play with them. Toys are at face level and not hanging below them.

- Moveable perches can swing in or out. Consequently the gym can fit into a compact space or be expanded.

- The design is readily customized with different perches and attachments.

- PVC is easy to clean, disinfect, and maintain. It is dishwasher safe.

- The Practically-Perfect-PAS is sturdy, lightweight, and easy to move with or without casters. It can be used indoors or out.

The Practically-Perfect-PAS is a wonderful gym to customize for a handicapped parrot. The design can be easily altered to accommodate special-needs birds.

Wrapping perches with jute or cohesive flexible bandage makes for a surer grip for birds missing feet or toes. Lauren's amazon Paco is missing his left foot and part of his leg. She laid a metal grate over the perching surfaces of her **Standard** gym to give Paco a flat surface on which to stand. Customized toy holders held parrot toys at lower levels for him. Eventually Paco was so comfortable with the setup that he would lay on his back on the grate and play with his parrot toys.

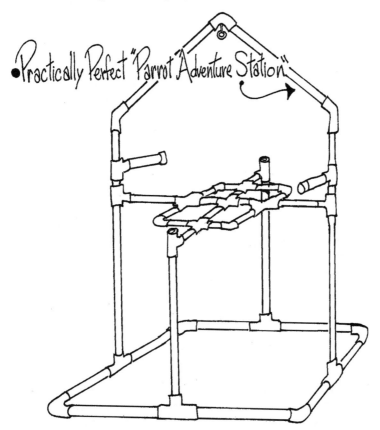

•Practically Perfect "Parrot Adventure Station"

For simplicity, shown with only Apex Parrot-Toy Holder

Oh, My Aching Feet

Parrots need perches of varying diameters and textures to help them maintain healthy feet. Spending 24 hours a day clinging to a perch can make for some tired tootsies. Customizing the perching surfaces on the Practically-Perfect-PAS is easy. *Perching surfaces* on the gym refer to the center of the gym on which the parrot walks, plus the perches themselves.

Sanding with coarse sandpaper or a belt sander can rough up some of the PVC perching surfaces to make gripping easier. By applying heavy pressure with a sander, you can actually "scallop" the PVC surfaces. Wooden dowels or natural branches can be substituted for some or all of the PVC perches. Anchor these dowels or branches with screws drilled up through the bottom of the PVC connectors if they don't fit tightly. It may also be possible to find a concrete conditioning perch that will fit into a connector. Wrapping some of the PVC perches with jute (we'll explain how to do this later) makes a wonderful, natural looking perch that is comfy on the feet. Cohesive flexible bandage (Vetrap™; Co-flex™) can also be used to wrap perching surfaces. This can be purchased at vet supply stores and large pet shops.

What Size Are You?

There are two sizes of Practically-Perfect-PAS to choose from. The Standard size gym can be constructed with either 1-, ¾-, or ½-inch perching surfaces and the **Large** gym with 1¼- inch perching surfaces.

Refer to the descriptions on the next page to choose the appropriate size gym for your parrot. We recommend that you read through the directions for the PAS first. You may decide to customize your parrot's gym and will have to change your shopping list accordingly. These gyms are floor models. Directions for the **Hookbill Haven**—a tabletop model for small parrots—will be found later in the chapter.

The approximate overall dimensions of the **Standard** gym are 30 inches square and 5 feet tall. The approximate overall dimensions of the **Large** gym are 42 inches square and 6 feet tall. The height of the gyms can vary if you change the lengths of the Apex of the Parrot-Toy Holder uprights as you will see from the directions. The height of the actual play area for your bird is 3 to 4 feet and because of the design of the gym they should not be able to climb to the top of the Apex.

There are four gyms from which to choose:

STANDARD SIZE 1-inch – **Standard size** gym with 1-inch perching surfaces—suitable for African Greys, amazons, small cockatoos, Eclectus, large conures, small macaws, and any parrot that finds a 1-inch perch comfortable.

STANDARD SIZE 3/4-inch – **Standard size** gym with ¾-inch perching surfaces—suitable for Timnehs, small amazons, small cockatoos, conures, pionus, lories, mini macaws and any other parrot that finds a ¾-inch perch comfortable.

STANDARD SIZE 1/2-inch – **Standard size** gym with ½-inch perching surfaces—suitable for cockatiels, Senegals, Jardines and the rest of the Poicephalus, the smallest conures, lorikeets, Quakers, and any other parrot that finds a ½-inch perch comfortable.

LARGE SIZE – **Large size** gym with 1¼-inch perching surfaces—suitable for large cockatoos, macaws, and any other parrot that finds a 1¼-inch perch comfortable.

If you are somewhat unsure about your "mechanical" abilities, do not despair! PVC is easy to work with. If you cut incorrectly or find that over time something doesn't work for you and your parrot, it is a simple matter to redo a piece, or section, of the gym.

Note: All connectors are <u>unthreaded</u>. When purchasing screweyes, be sure the "eye" is large enough to accept the quick links that you use on your parrot toys. When drilling holes in the PVC for the screweyes, use a drill bit that is slightly smaller than the screw for a tight fit.

NOTES & SKETCHES

GYM SHOPPING LISTS:

- **Standard Gym with 1-inch Perch**

- **Standard Gym with 3/4-inch Perch**

- **Standard Gym with 1/2-inch Perch**

- **Large Gym**

Standard Gym w/ 1" Perching Surface   Cost: $25-35   **Notes:**

☐   32 ½ feet of 1-inch PVC.

☐   4 additional feet of 1-inch PVC or the equivalent in wooden dowels or natural branches for perches. For ease in buying wooden dowels, take a connector with you to check the fit.

☐   ten 1-inch 90° elbow connectors

☐   thirteen 1-inch 3-way connectors

☐   five 1-inch 4-way connectors

☐   two 1-inch 45° elbow connectors

☐   one 1-inch cap to top the Spiral Steps and up to six additional caps depending on how many perches you will make from the PVC.

☐   screweyes for hanging parrot toys, swings, etc.

Standard Gym w/ ¾-inch Perching Surface Cost: $20-25

☐   25 ½ feet of 1-inch PVC

☐   7 feet of ¾-inch PVC

☐   4 additional feet of ¾-inch PVC or the equivalent in wooden dowels or natural branches for perches. For ease in buying wooden dowels, take a connector with you to check the fit.

☐   five 1-inch 90° elbow connectors

☐   four ¾-inch 90° elbow connectors

☐   one 1x¾-inch 90° reducing elbow connector

Notes:

- ☐ four 1-inch 3-way connectors

- ☐ nine 1x1x¾- inch reducing 3-way connectors

- ☐ five ¾ inch 4-way connectors

- ☐ two 1-inch 45° elbow connectors

- ☐ one 1-inch cap to top the spiral steps and up to 6 additional ¾-inch caps depending on how many perches you will make from the PVC.

- ☐ screweyes for hanging parrot toys, swings, etc.

Standard Gym w/ ½" Perching Surface   **Cost: $10-20**

- ☐ 25 ½ feet of 1-inch PVC

- ☐ 7 feet of ½-inch PVC

- ☐ 4 additional feet of ½-inch PVC or the equivalent in wooden dowel or natural branches for perches. For ease in buying wooden dowel, take a connector with you to check the fit.

- ☐ five 1-inch 90° elbow connectors

- ☐ four ½-inch 90° elbow connectors

- ☐ one 1x½-inch 90° reducing elbow connector

- ☐ four 1-inch 3-way connectors

- ☐ nine 1x1x ½-inch reducing 3-way connectors

- ☐ five ½-inch 4-way connectors

- ☐ two 1-inch 45° elbow connectors

❒ one 1-inch cap to top the Spiral Steps and up to six additional ½-inch caps depending on how many perches you will make from the PVC.

❒ screweyes for hanging parrot toys, swings, etc.

Notes:

Large Gym   Cost: $40-50

❒ 42 feet 1¼-inch PVC

❒ 6 additional feet of 1¼-inch PVC or the equivalent in wooden dowels or natural branches for perches. For ease in buying wooden dowels, take a connector with you to check the fit.

❒ ten 1¼-inch 90° elbow connectors

❒ thirteen 1¼-inch 3-way connectors

❒ five 1¼-inch 4-way connectors

❒ two 1¼-inch 45° elbow connectors

❒ one 1¼-inch cap to top the Spiral Steps and up to 6 additional caps depending on how many perches you will make from the PVC.

❒ screweyes for hanging parrot toys, swings, etc.

❒ If you are constructing the Large gym, skip ahead to page 105 for assembly instructions.

DIRECTIONS FOR ASSEMBLING STANDARD GYMS:

- **Base and Leg Assembly**

- **Perching Surface Assembly**

- **Toppers Assembly**

Don't be intimidated by these shopping lists. Any well-supplied hardware store should have the parts you need. Some of the large hardware retailers even color code the sizes of connectors. Really stumped? Hand the list to the sales associate and let him or her do the picking for you.

Each gym consists of three sections and can be built in this order:

- The **Base and Legs** are the same for all three of the **Standard** size gyms. They will be constructed of 1-inch PVC.

- The **Perching Surfaces** consist of the **support cross** and **inner square**. This area of the gym will be constructed from either 1-, ¾-, or ½-diameter PVC depending on which gym you have chosen.

- The **toppers** consist of the **Apex Parrot Toy/Swing Holder**, the **Spiral Steps**, and the **Basic Perch**. The basic construction of these parts will be from 1-inch PVC on all three of the gyms. The perches will be either 1-, ¾-, or ½-inch diameter depending which gym you have chosen.

Notes:

Notes:

Start with the Base and Legs First:

☐   8 feet of 1-inch PVC cut into eight 1-foot sections for the base

☐   12 feet of 1-inch PVC cut into four 3-foot sections for the legs

☐   four 1-inch 90° elbow connectors for the base.

☐   eight 1-inch 3-way connectors

1. Cut all sections of pipe first. 2. Connect the 1-foot sections to the elbows and 3-way connectors as shown in the diagram below. 3. Push the legs into the top of the 3-way connectors. 4. Place the 3-way connectors on top of the four legs with the center holes facing the middle of the gym. The base will form a square with elbows at the corners and the legs coming from the *center* of each section.

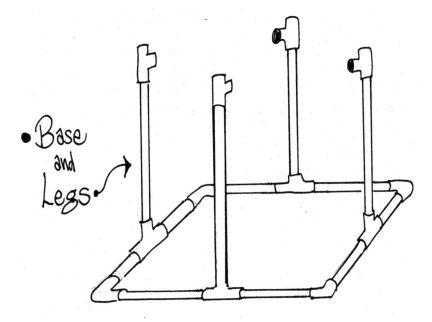

• Base and Legs

Perching Surfaces for the Standard Gym:

If you are making the **Standard** 1-inch gym you will be using all 1-inch connectors. If you are building either the ¾- or ½-inch gym, you will use the **reducing connectors** you bought so that you can connect the smaller diameter PVC to the 1-inch pipe that forms the legs. Instructions for *assembling* the perching surfaces will be the same for all three sizes. As mentioned previously, we recommend that all PVC that is used for perching be sanded, scalloped, or wrapped in jute. Directions for wrapping perches with jute will be found in the section on customizing your gym and can be done after the gym is completed.

Support Cross

☐   3½ feet of 1-inch PVC cut into eight 5 ¼-inch sections. Sand and/or scallop now. Wrapping in jute can be done after assembling.

☐   five 1-inch 4-way connectors

1.   Using the 5¼-inch sections and the 4-way connectors, construct a cross as shown in the diagram on the next page.

Inner Square

☐   3½ feet of 1-inch PVC cut into eight 5 ¼-inch sections. Sand and/or scallop now. Wrapping in jute can be done after assembling.

☐   four 1" 90° elbow connectors

Notes: 1. Using the 5¼-inch sections and the 90° elbows as corners, construct a square as shown in the diagram below. 2. The inner square is a tight fit especially the last sections. You may have to manipulate the pieces to get the last ones secure. At this point, you should have a sturdy structure on which to put your **Toppers**.

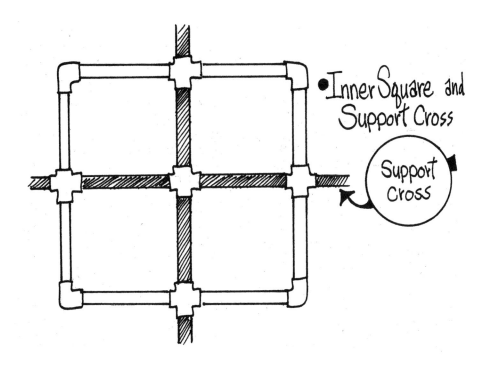

Toppers for the Standard Gym:

Apex Parrot Toy and Swing Holder
Before beginning construction of the **Apex**, you will need to decide what you wish to hang from the top. This could be a swing, spiral perch, thick rope, or a parrot toy.

This will determine the length of the upright pieces you will cut. If it is a ring swing or spiral perch, be sure it is low enough that your parrot can climb on to it from the nearby perches. Uprights of 2 to 4 inches usually work for most things.

❒   4 feet of 1-inch PVC cut into two 17-inch sections for the apex, two 2- to 4-inch sections for the uprights, and two 2-inch sections ("joiners").

❒   If you will be using PVC for perches, cut two perches 5- to 6-inch in length from the remaining pipe. Sand or scallop if desired. You can also use a wooden dowel cut to the appropriate lengths. If you use a dowel, during assembly drill a hole up through the bottom of the connector into the dowel and anchor the perch with a screw.

❒   two 1-inch 3-way connectors, two 1-inch 45° elbow connectors, one 1-inch 90° elbow connector, and two 1-inch caps.

The **Apex** will span the top of the gym. 1. Place one of the 2-inch sections into the top of one of the 3-way connectors on the legs. 2. Place the other 2-inch section on the 3-way connector across from the first one. 3. Place a 3-way connector on top of each of these. (These little 2-inch "joiners" attach two connectors with no added height.) 4. Assemble the rest of the pieces as shown in the diagram on the next page. The top connector is a 90° elbow. 5. Drill a hole in the bend of the 90° connector and insert the screweye. 6. Place screweyes anywhere else you wish to hang parrot toys or swings.

Notes:

*Note: We do not recommend wrapping the **Apex** Parrot-Toy Holder in jute or cohesive flexible bandage as this might allow your parrot to climb up to the top of the **Apex** and sit above your head.*

For those of you constructing the ¾- or ½-inch gyms, use the reducing 3-way connectors (1 x1 x ¾-inch or 1x1x½-inch) on top of the 2-inch joiners. This will allow you to use the smaller diameter perch. All measurements remain the same.

Spiral Steps

☐   one foot of 1-inch PVC cut into three 2-inch sections and one 4-inch section

☐   three 8-inch perches of PVC, dowel, or natural branch. Sand or scallop the PVC if desired

☐   one 1-inch cap and three more (optional) if you are using PVC for perches

☐   three 1-inch 3-way connectors

1. Choose one of the two remaining empty 3-way connectors on the legs. 2. Alternate 2-inch joiner sections with the 3-way connectors (the connector may touch) and top the Spiral with the 4-inch piece and the cap. 3. Attach perches and caps to the 3-way connectors. 4. Stagger the steps to form a spiral.

For those of you constructing the ¾- or ½-inch gyms, use the **reducing** 3-way connectors (1-inch x 1-inch x ¾-inch or 1-inch x 1-inch x ½-inch) on the Spiral Steps. All measurements remain the same.

Ohhh....I love the variety of views!

Spiral Steps

Notes:

Basic Perch

☐   one 2-inch section of 1-inch PVC

☐   one 10 to 12-inch section of PVC, dowel, or natural branch to be used as a perch

☐   one 1-inch 90° elbow connector and one 1-inch cap

1. In the last 3-way connector place a 2-inch joiner and attach the 90° elbow. The elbow connector and the 3-way connector should touch. 2. Attach the perch to this and cap it.

For those of you constructing the ¾- or ½-inch gyms, use the reducing 90° elbow connector (1x1x¾-inch or 1x1x ½-inch) on the basic perch. All measurements remain the same.

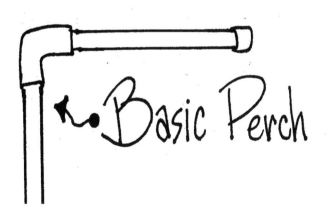

Congratulations! You have now completed the Practically -
Perfect-Parrot Adventure Station. Add a Splat Mat, parrot toys,
a swing, your feathered buddy and let the fun begin!

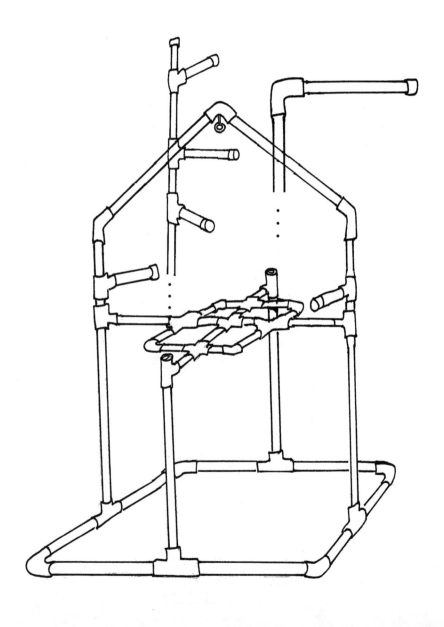

DIRECTIONS FOR ASSEMBLING LARGE GYM:

- **Base and Leg Assembly**

- **Perching Surface Assembly**

- **Toppers Assembly**

The Large Practically-Perfect-PAS offers tons of fun for the big guys. Read on…

The **large gym**, which is suitable for large macaws and cockatoos, consists of four sections and can be built in this order:

- The **base and legs** will be constructed of 1¼-inch PVC.

- The **perching surfaces** consist of the **support cross** and **inner square**. For the Large gym this area will be constructed from 1¼-inch diameter PVC.

- The **toppers** consist of the **apex parrot toy and swing holder**, the **spiral steps**, and the **basic perch**. The apex will be constructed from 1¼-inch PVC. You can vary the diameter and material of the perches if you choose.

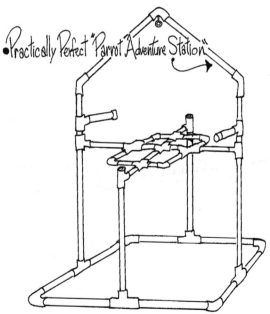

Practically Perfect "Parrot Adventure Station"

For simplicity shown with only Apex Parrot-Toy Holder

Notes:

Start with the Base and Legs First:

- ☐ 12 feet of 1 ¼-inch PVC cut into eight 1 ½-foot sections for the base

- ☐ 12 feet of 1¼-inch PVC cut into four 3-foot sections for the legs

- ☐ four 1¼-inch 90° elbow connectors for the base

- ☐ eight 1¼-inch 3-way connectors

1. Cut all sections of pipe first. 2. Connect the 1½-foot sections to the elbows and 3-way connectors as shown in the diagram below. 3. Push the legs into the top of the 3-way connectors. 4. Place the 3-way connectors on top of the legs with the center holes facing the middle of the gym. The base will form a square with elbows at the corners and the legs coming up from the *center* of each section.

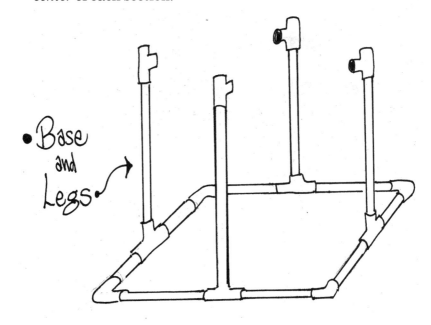

• Base and Legs•

Perching Surfaces for the Large Gym:

The Large gym uses all 1¼-inch connectors. We recommend that all PVC that is used for perching be sanded, scalloped (created by heavy pressure on your belt sander), or wrapped in jute. Directions for wrapping PVC with jute will be found in the section on customizing your gym and can be done after the gym is completed.

Support Cross

❑   5 feet of 1¼-inch PVC cut into eight 7½-inch sections. Sand or scallop if desired.

❑   five 1¼-inch 4-way connectors

1. Using the 7½-inch sections and the 4-way connectors, construct a cross as shown in the diagram.

Inner Square

❑   5 feet of 1¼-inch PVC cut into eight 7 ½-inch sections. Sand or scallop if desired

❑   four 1¼-inch 90° elbow connectors

1. Using the 7½-inch sections and the 90° elbows as corners, construct a square as shown in the diagram on the next page.
2. The inner square is a tight fit especially the last sections. You may have to manipulate the pieces to get the last ones secure. At this point, you should have a sturdy structure on which to put your **Toppers**.

Notes:

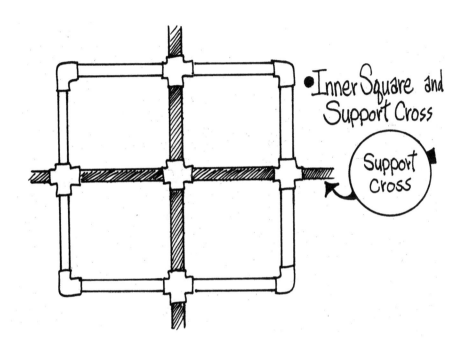

Toppers for Large Gym

Apex Parrot-Toy/Swing Holder

☐ 6 feet of 1¼-inch PVC cut into two 24-inch sections for the Apex, two 7½-inch sections for the uprights, and two 2-inch joiner sections

☐ If you will be using PVC for perches, cut two perches 8 to 9 inches in length. Sand or scallop if desired. You can also use a wooden dowel cut to the appropriate lengths. If you use a dowel, during assembly drill a hole up through the bottom of the connector into the dowel and anchor the perch with a screw.

☐ two 1¼-inch 3-way connectors, two 1¼-inch 45° elbow connectors, one 1¼-inch 90° elbow connector, and two 1¼-inch caps if you use PVC perches

1. The **Apex** will span the top of the gym. Place one of the 2-inch sections into the top of one of the 3-way connectors on the legs. 2. Place the other 2-inch section on the 3-way connector across from the first one. 3. Place a 3-way connector on top each of these. (These little 2-inch "joiners" attach two connectors with no added height.) 4. Assemble the rest of the pieces as shown in the diagram on the next page. The top connector is a 90° elbow. 5. Drill a hole in the bend of the 90° connector and insert the screweye. 6. Place screweyes anywhere else you wish to hang parrot toys or swings.

*Note: We do not recommend wrapping the **Apex** Parrot-Toy Holder in jute or cohesive flexible bandage as this might allow your parrot to climb up to the top of the **Apex** and sit above your head.*

Notes:

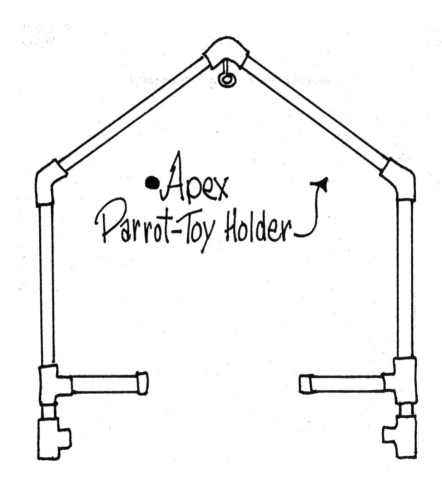

Spiral Steps

❑   14 inches of 1¼-inch PVC cut into three 4-inch sections and one 2-inch ("joiner") section.

❑   Cut three 9-inch perches of 1¼-inch PVC, dowel, or natural branch. Sand or scallop the PVC if desired.

❑   one 1¼-inch cap for the top and three more (optional) if you use PVC for your perches

❑   three 1¼-inch 3-way connectors

1. Choose one of the two remaining empty 3-way connectors on the legs and put the 2-inch "joiner" on it. 2. Place a 3-way connector next. 3. Alternate the remaining 4-inch sections and 3-way connectors. 4. Place a cap on the last 4-inch piece. 5. Attach perches and caps, or dowels to the 3-way connectors. 6. Stagger the steps to form a spiral.

Ohhh...I love the variety of views!

Spiral Steps

Notes:

Basic Perch

☐   4 inches of 1¼-inch PVC and a 16-inch section of either 1¼-inch PVC, dowel, or natural branch to be used as a perch

☐   one 1¼-inch 90° elbow connector and one 1¼-inch cap

1. In the last 3-way connector place the 4-inch section. 2. Attach the 90° elbow and attach the perch to this. 3. Cap the perch.

Congratulations! You have now completed the large Practically-Perfect-Parrot Adventure Station. Add a splat mat, some mega-parrot toys, a gonzo swing, your feathered dynamo, and get ready for some avian action!

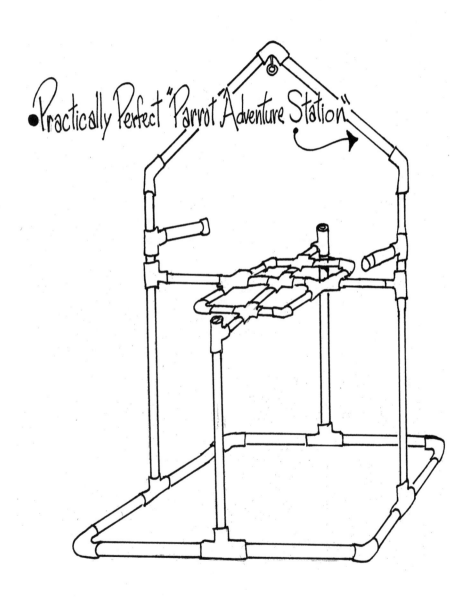

THE
HOOKBILL HAVEN:

- **Shopping List**

- **Base and Legs Assembly**

- **Perching Surface Assembly**

- **Toppers Assembly**

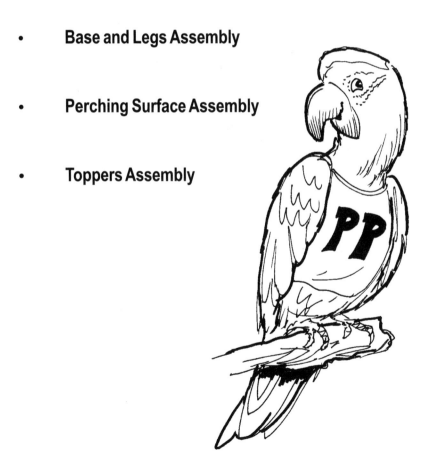

Want a Parrot Adventure Station for the little guys that will fit on the table? Try the **Hookbill Haven**.

This tabletop model uses ½-inch PVC so it will be suitable for the Poicephalus, conures, Quakers, ringnecks, cockatiels, and any other parrot that finds a ½-inch perch comfortable. The directions follow:

Shopping List for the Hookbill Haven   **Cost $5-10**

❒   13 feet of ½-inch PVC

❒   2 additional feet of ½-inch PVC or the equivalent in wooden dowels or branches for perches

❒   eleven ½-inch 3-way connectors

❒   seven ½-inch 90° elbow connectors

❒   two ½-inch 45° elbow connectors

❒   up to three ½-inch caps if you will be using PVC perches

❒   screweyes for hanging parrot toys

Notes:

Base and Legs for the Hookbill Haven:

☐ 4 feet of PVC cut into eight 6-inch sections for the base

☐ Decide on the height of the legs. Cut 1½ to 3 feet of PVC into four 4- to 8-inch sections for the legs. If you want longer legs, adjust the amounts needed accordingly.

☐ four 90° elbow connectors for the base

☐ four 3-way connectors

1. Connect the 6-inch sections to the elbows and 3-way connectors as shown in the diagram below. 2. Push the legs into the tops of the 3-way connectors. The base will form a square with the elbows at the corners and the legs coming up from the center of each section.

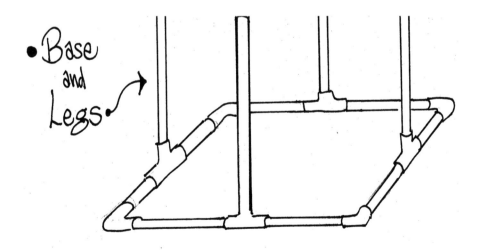

• Base and Legs •

Perching Surfaces for the Hookbill Haven:

The perching surfaces of the Hookbill Haven are shaped like the letter **"H."** Your bird will walk on this surface. The "H" as well as any perches constructed of PVC should be sanded, scalloped, or wrapped in jute. This will ensure good footing especially for the smaller parrots. Sanding is best done before assembly. Wrapping can be done after.

"H" Perching Surface

☐   1½ feet of PVC cut into four 4 ¼-inch sections for the sides of the "H"

☐   9 inches of PVC for the middle of the "H"

☐   six 3-way connectors

1. Place a 3-way connector on top of each of the four legs. As you can see from the diagram below, the "H" sits at an angle to the base. 2. Construct the sides using the 4 ¼-inch sections and 3-way connectors. 3. Span the middle with the 9-inch piece.

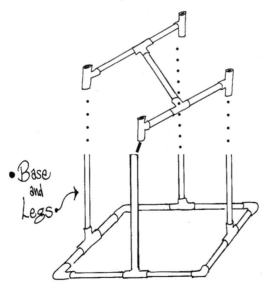

• Base and Legs

Notes:

Toppers for the Hookbill Haven:

The Toppers consist of an **Apex Parrot-Toy/Swing** Holder and two sets of perches. There are a couple of decisions you will need to make when constructing these. Decide what you want to hang from the apex as this will determine how high to make it. This might be a swing, spiral perch, knotted rope, or parrot toy. You will also need to decide if you want to use PVC, dowels, or branches for your perches. If you or your parrot change your minds later, it is easy to redo any of the parts.

Apex Parrot-Toy / Swing Holder

☐   3 feet of PVC cut into two 10-inch sections for the apex and two 4- to 8-inch sections for the uprights or longer depending on the height you have chosen.

☐   two 45° elbow connectors

☐   one 90° elbow connector

The apex will span the gym. 1. Place one of the uprights in one of the 3-way connectors and the other in the 3-way connector across from it. 2. Top each with a 45° elbow. 3. Add the 10"-inch sections. The top of the apex will be the 90° elbow connector. 4. Drill a hole and screw a screweye in the bend of the elbow connector to hang a parrot toy, swing, or spiral perch.

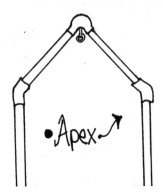

•Apex

Basic Perch

☐   Cut one 2-inch section of PVC

☐   one perch 6 to 8 inches of PVC, dowel, or natural branch

☐   one 90° elbow connector

☐   one cap if you are using a PVC perch

1. Place the 2-inch section of PVC into one of the remaining 3-way connectors. 2. Top it with the elbow connector and add the perch and cap. 3. If you use a dowel or branch that does not fit tightly into the connector, drill a hole up through the bottom of the connector and use a small wood screw to hold the perch in place.

Notes:

Double Perch

☐ Cut two 2-inch sections of PVC

☐ Cut two perches 6 to 8 inches of PVC, dowel, or natural branch

☐ one 3-way connector

☐ one 90°elbow connector

☐ two caps for the PVC perches

1. Place the 2-inch PVC section into the last 3-way connector. 2. Top it with a 3-way connector, the other 2-inch section, and the 90° elbow connector. 3. Add the two perches and caps. 4. If you didn't sand the PVC perches, wrap them in jute (the directions can be found in the next section). 5. Drill a hole and screw in a screweye wherever you want to hang a parrot toy or swing. Add a mini splat mat and a feathered friend and you're ready for adventure!

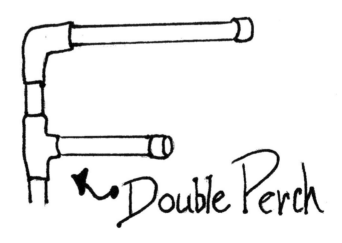

Double Perch

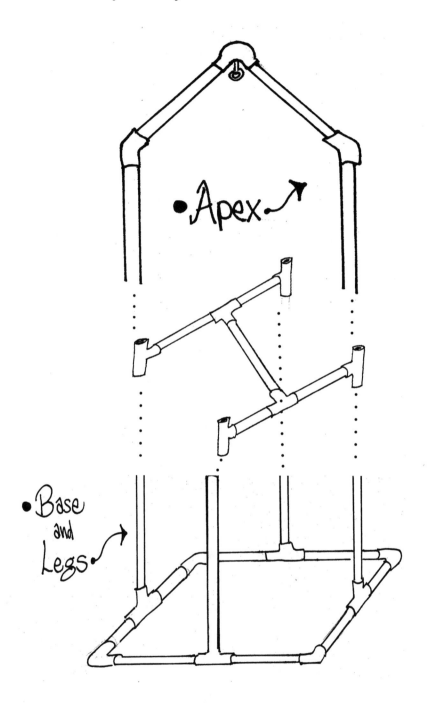

• Apex

• Base
and
Legs •

14 CUSTOMIZING YOUR "PRACTICALLY-PERFECT-PARROT-ADVENTURE STATION PLAYGYM"

Wrapping Perches in Jute—We advise purchasing jute at a hobby shop rather than the hardware store. Refer to the chapter on parrot toys for recommendations. Six-ply jute will work nicely for perch wrapping. The end of the perch that you *start* wrapping from will be the end that you ultimately cap. Don't start wrapping at the very end—leave some room for the cap. The end of the perch that you *finish* wrapping will go into the connector. This will be a tight fit because you will be catching part of the jute and you may need to tap it with a hammer or mallet.

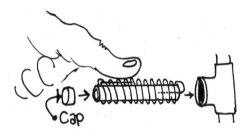

Lay about 4 inches of jute along the perch. Hold it in place with your thumb and begin wrapping towards you catching the piece of jute lying on the perch as you go. Wrap tightly and completely. Once you reach the end, leave about 4 extra inches and cut the jute. Push the extra up into the pipe holding the rest of the wrapping so that it does not unravel. Push this end into the connector. Cap the other end.

Adding Food Cups—Metal or plastic food cups that come with a bottom bolt can be attached to your gym by drilling through a PVC or wooden dowel perch. If your bird will be spending considerable time out on his PAS, consider adding two cups, one for food and one for water. Be sure to place them where they won't be soiled by droppings. A **cup holder** can be constructed as shown below:

Adding Casters—Wheels can easily be added to your PAS. You will need 3 feet of 1 x 2 pine board and four casters. Cut the 1 x 2 at an angle to fit under the corners of the base. Screw casters to the 1 x 2 pieces. Attach the boards with casters to the corners of the base as shown in the diagram below by screwing up through the wood and into the PVC pipe.

Notes:

Want to customize even further?
The toppers on the next few pages can be substituted for the ones described in the gym instructions above. Use the appropriate diameter PVC and connectors for your size Practically-Perfect-PAS.

1. Adding a "Tree"—An interesting branch of parrot-safe wood can be wedged into the top of one of the 3-way connectors on the legs. This could take the place of the basic perch or the spiral steps.

2. Parrot-Toy Holder

You will need:
☐   one 90° elbow; 18- to 34-inch PVC pipe depending on the size of your bird; one screweye

☐   Construct this from 1-inch PVC for the Standard gym and 1¼-inch PVC for the Large gym. The upright can be from 10 to 18 inches depending on the height of your parrot. The idea is not to make it so low that your parrot can sit on top of it. The crosspiece that holds the parrot toy should measure from 8 to 16 inches. Don't make this piece too long or the weight of the pipe itself and the parrot toy hanging from it will cause it to pull out. As an extra precaution, you can drill up through the connector and pipe and insert a screw. Add a screweye and you're all set!

Parrot Toy Holder

3. Parrot-Toy Holder with Perch

This is the parrot toy holder previously described above with the addition of a perch.

You will need:

☐ In addition to the materials listed for the Parrot-Toy Holder, you will also need one 3-way connector (if your parrot is using a ¾- or ½-inch perch, you will need a **reducing connector**); 5 to 9 inches of PVC or the equivalent in a wooden dowel for the perch; one 2-inch piece of PVC ("joiner"); and one cap if you are using a PVC perch.

☐ The 2-inch joiner will attach the 3-way connector to the gym. Continue constructing the parrot toy holder as previously described. Add the perch.

Parrot Toy Holder w/perch

Notes:

4. Flat-Top Parrot-Toy Holder with Perches—This Parrot-Toy Holder can take the place of the Apex Parrot-Toy Holder. It will span the top of the gym.

You will need:

☐ two 90° elbow connectors; two 3-way connectors; 4 ½ feet of 1-inch PVC for the Standard gym or 6½ feet of 1¼-inch PVC for the Large gym; and 2 caps. If you are using wooden dowels or natural branches for the perches, omit 1 foot of the 1-inch PVC or 1½ feet of the 1¼-inch PVC and the 2 caps.

☐ For the Standard gym you will need to cut two 2-inch joiners; two uprights 12 to 14 inches; and one cross piece of 23 inches. You can adjust the uprights making them taller or shorter to suit your parrot and the type of parrot toys or swing you wish to hang from the crosspiece. The perches can be 5 to 6 inches in length or longer if you desire.

☐ For the Large gym you will need to cut two 2-inch joiners; two uprights 18 to 20 inches; and one cross piece of 35 inches. You can adjust the uprights depending on the size of your parrot and the type of parrot toys or swing you wish to hang. Perches can be 8 to 9 inches or longer.

•Flat-Top Parrot-Toy Holder w/perches•

Cool!

5. Swing—(can be used with the Flat-Top Parrot-Toy Holder) The directions below are for a small, medium, and large swing. Be sure to use a diameter of PVC pipe that is comfortable for your parrot to grip. *It is important to provide secure footing on the swing by sanding, scalloping, or wrapping in jute.* The dimensions given are suggestions. You may wish to change the measurements to suit your particular pet bird.

Notes:

You will need:

☐   **Small**—2 feet of ½- or ¾-inche diameter PVC pipe cut into two 9-inch sections and one 7-inch section, two 90°elbow connectors, two end caps, four screweyes, and two "S" hooks.

☐   **Medium**—31 inches of ¾- or 1-inch diameter PVC pipe cut into two 11-inch sections and one 9-inch section, two 90° elbow connectors, two end caps, four screweyes, and two "S" hooks.

☐   **Large**—42 inches of 1- or 1¼-inch diameter PVC pipe cut into two 15-inch sections and one 12-inch section, two 90° elbow connectors, two end caps, four screweyes, and two "S" hooks.

Assemble the swing as shown in the diagram below. Be sure the pieces fit snuggly. For added safety, you may want to cement or screw the end caps in place.

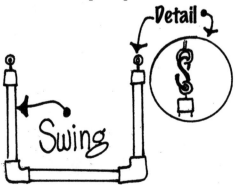

Thank You... for taking time to read this book.
PP
Now if you'll excuse me... it's my playtime!

AFTERWORD

We hope you had as much fun reading *Parrot Toys and Play Areas* as we had writing it.

Our goal was to motivate and excite you to expand your feathered friend's horizons and to realize the critical role that parrot-toys and play areas play in the life of your bird. We encourage you to share ideas and learn from other individual pet bird owners and bird clubs. Companion parrot publications such as *Bird Talk* and the *Pet Bird Report* offer information on parrot-toy and play area dealers. There are many companies out there that craft their products with much love and care. The Internet too provides a wealth of information on parrot-toys and related merchandise. Always remember that you are the one who has the final say on what play products are right for your feathered companion.

Have Fun!
Carol D'Arezzo and Lauren Shannon-Nunn

Contact Us At: info@practicalparrot.com

Parrot Toys and Play Areas: How To Put Some Fun Into Your Parrot's Life is the first book in the *Practical Parrot Guide Series*. Be watching for the next one.

A FINAL THOUGHT.......

We would like to propose to all of you who love and enjoy your bird to **go beyond your living room** and become an advocate for parrots. Just doing one of the things listed below could make a difference in the life of one of these incredible feathered creatures.

- Share information and advice with other parrot owners.

- Help educate a novice parrot owner.

- Give a donation to those researching avian diseases.

- Give a donation to those doing research that provides insight into psittacine intelligence and behavior.

- Give a donation or work for conservation efforts to preserve parrot habitats.

- Donate money, time, or supplies to individuals and organizations that provide rescue and sanctuary for parrots.

- Speak up *anywhere* you see parrots being kept in abusive or neglectful conditions.

- Learn about legislation that affects you as a pet bird owner.

- Join a bird club, conservation, or aviculture organization and become involved.

- If you can make the commitment, take in another parrot that needs a home.

- Support and recommend good veterinarians, ethical retail establishments and breeders, and companies that make quality parrot products.

ABOUT THE AUTHORS

Carol D'Arezzo was "found" by an escapee cockatiel over ten years ago and has never been the same since. Her feathered family, many acquired through rescue, now includes four macaws, two cockatoos, four African Greys, an amazon, an Eclectus, and a lively bunch of smaller parrots including the original cockatiel, "Cinco".

She lectures and consults on parrot behavior with an emphasis on practical solutions to problems and long-term commitment.

Birds of all kinds fascinate Carol. For eight years she co-owned and operated a retail store, Wild Birds Unlimited, in Colorado Springs, Colorado, that catered to the hobby of backyard birdfeeding. She lectured extensively in the community on backyard birds and the methods to attract them.

As a small business owner she has consulted and worked with other small businesses in the areas of accounting and customer service.

Carol holds a B.S. in Biology and has taught biology and science in the Aurora, Colorado public schools. She is a PIJAC Certified Avian Specialist. She now resides with her flock and two Bichons in Virginia where she works in real estate and writes.

Lauren Shannon-Nunn has been an animal lover for as long as she can remember. One of her first jobs was as a sales associate and head kennel manager for a pet shop selling a variety of animals including parrots.

For several years Lauren worked for and eventually managed a "M.A.P." certified aviary in Colorado. She was responsible for the raising and socialization of young parrots.

One task that she particularly enjoyed was assisting customers in deciding which parrot species would be most appropriate for them and their lifestyle.

Her feathered family consists of "Pebbles" a slender-billed conure, "Paco" an amazon who is missing part of one leg, and five lively parakeets.

Lauren is a graduate of Berry College in Rome, Georgia. She resides in Colorado where she runs her petsitting and parrot behavior consulting business, "Under One Wing". She is a PIJAC Certified Avian Specialist.

INDEX

A

Acrobats 11
African Grey 10, 30
Amazon 10, 14
Apex 86, 88, 96, 100, 101, 106, 110, 119, 127
apex 100, 106, 119
Apex Parrot-Toy Holder 101
Apex Parrot-Toy/Swing Holder 110

B

baffle 50, 73
Base and Legs 96
beak 3-5, 11, 17, 18, 24, 36, 43, 49, 52, 55
Bird in a Basket 77
bird marts 4
biting and chewing 5
Buzz-Saw 12, 13
Buzz-saw 11

C

Chew 3, 32
chew 3-7, 10-13, 15, 17, 20, 30, 33, 36, 39, 43, 44, 51-55, 57
Chewing 3
  wood chips 13
cleaning 15
Closed-link chain 17
cockatiel 13, 23, 24, 37, 49, 57
cockatoo 3, 5, 6, 10, 24, 38, 54, 55, 67, 69, 75, 88, 106
companion bird 4
corrugated boxes 11
costume jewelry 18
cotton rope 17
Cuddlers 22
  Coconut Hideaway 23
cuddling 20
cup holder 124

D

Destructibles 30

Food Chews 32
Get Colorful 33
Go Natural 32
destructibles 30, 31, 32

E

Eclectus 3, 10, 25

F

Feeding activities 4
flock 4, 9, 66, 67, 71, 74, 75, 76
Food Finders 38, 56
  Coconut Surprise 40
  Crunchy Roll 40
  Peek-a-Treat 39
  Rawhide-a-Nut 39
  Roll-o'-Treat 41
  Spoon Treats 40
Foot Toys 13, 52-54
  Crunchies 53
  Let's Go Shopping 53
  Silly Sacks 53

G

Gabriel Foundation 16
Gatherers 11
gym 61, 65, 66, 67, 72, 73, 77, 79, 80, 81, 83, 85-89, 94, 96, 97, 98, 100-103, 106-108, 110, 119, 123, 125-127

H

HeadMate 62
hemp 17
Hide and Seekers 12
homemade parrot-toy 8
Hookbill Haven 88, 115-119
Hookbill Hodgepodge 78

I

Instant Little Bird PAS 77

J

Jingle bells 18
jungle 14
jute 14, 17

The Book You and Your Parrot Have Been Waiting For

Check Your Leading Bookstore
OR
Order Right Here

☐ YES, I want _____ copies of *Parrot Toys and Play Areas* at $16.95 each, plus $3.50 shipping for the first book and $.50 for each additional book.(Virginia residents add 4.5% sales tax). Please allow 15 days for delivery.

My check or money order for $_____ is enclosed.
Please charge my:
☐ **MASTERCARD**   ☐ **VISA**   ☐ **AMERICAN EXPRESS**

Name _____

Organization _____

Address _____

City/State/Zip _____

Phone _____ E-mail _____

Card # _____ Exp. Date _____

Signature _____

Please make checks payable and return to:
CrowFire Publishing
PO Box 2456
Springfield, VA 22152-2456

Call your credit card orders to: 800-431-1579

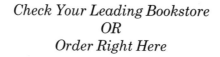

The Book You and Your Parrot Have Been Waiting For

Check Your Leading Bookstore
OR
Order Right Here

❐ YES, I want ____ copies of *Parrot Toys and Play Areas* at $16.95 each, plus $3.50 shipping for the first book and $.50 for each additional book.(Virginia residents add 4.5% sales tax). Please allow 15 days for delivery.

My check or money order for $_____ is enclosed.
Please charge my:
❐ **MASTERCARD** ❐ **VISA** ❐ **AMERICAN EXPRESS**

Name _____

Organization _____

Address _____

City/State/Zip _____

Phone _____ E-mail _____

Card # _____ Exp. Date _____

Signature _____

Please make checks payable and return to:
CrowFire Publishing
PO Box 2456
Springfield, VA 22152-2456

Call your credit card orders to: 800-431-1579